From
THE MASTER'S HAND
TO MINE

BEARING FRUIT THROUGH CONVERSATIONS WITH GOD

K a t h y   M .   C r o u c h

ISBN 978-1-63961-940-5 (paperback)
ISBN 978-1-63961-941-2 (digital)

Christian Faith Publishing
832 Park Avenue
Meadville, PA 16335
www.christianfaithpublishing.com

Printed in the United States of America

CONTENTS

PREFACE

I believe that God speaks to us in many different ways. Have you ever considered the fact that a prayer is an actual conversation with God? Do you expect answers when you have questions? These questions are what inspired me to write this book. As you turn the pages, you will find God's voice embedded into our twenty-two conversations ninety-three times, and through the Scriptures, he helps me understand and deal with many different and oftentimes difficult topics.

I love working in the yard. I live in the Carolinas where the pine trees keep me busy raking, and if I have picked up one pinecone in my lifetime, I have picked up ten thousand. It is an endless task; however, it is where I love to be. I talk to God while I'm working. A few months ago, I heard from God in a way I cannot explain. He clearly nudged me to go record our conversation, so I dropped the rake, grabbed my computer, and started typing. That was the first conversation of many that would follow. I bring my questions and concerns to him, and he whispers back to me the things I need to hear.

After writing many conversations, I began to wonder what God's plan for these might be. I have taught high school students in Sunday school for forty years. Recently, I had been looking for a new curriculum or just something that would be relevant for these teens living in a world that I feel has truly lost its way. God immediately placed it upon my heart to do something with these conversations. It is my belief that when God leads you to do something for his kingdom, he will take care of the rest. It's not so much about the success of it, but it is about going and doing. It is about being obedient, so I went.

I am currently using this curriculum with my teens to pilot this endeavor. Their feedback not only inspires me, but they help me work out all of the kinks in the process. After we read a conversation, the students immediately write down their reflections on it. These conversations capture their attention from the very beginning and keep them motivated throughout the lesson. Each conversation begins by asking questions to get those creative juices flowing, and then we read Scripture together that is actually embedded inside of the conversation. It is amazing to observe these students as they actually see and hear God's Word in a different setting. It helps them understand how easily God communicates with us.

God has used me to teach these young adults how to hear his voice during these uncertain times we are living in. The students receive a copy of the scriptures to carry with them. I encourage them to read them and commit them to memory.

My vision for this material is broad. I envision it being used to teach teen youth groups, teen or older adult Sunday school, individual Bible study, retreats, small group discipleship lessons, and so much more. It could be used for adults from ages fifteen to ninety-five. These conversations can be used to build a firm foundation because they deal with everyday life experiences. I am a writer of poetry, so at the end of each lesson, I include a poem to wrap things up.

The people in the conversations are all family members. They were often the inspiration I needed as I talked with God.

I am excited to see where the Lord will take this. It is my prayer that it will indeed bear fruit in the lives of all who read it.

Kathy M. Crouch

ACKNOWLEDGMENTS

My first conversation began when I expressed to God my love for Psalm 46:10. "Be still and know that I am God" is my favorite verse, and it was the foundation upon which the conversations began and this curriculum was built. This endeavor is truly a gift from the Master's hand to mine. God is the author; he just used me to pen the words.

There are many people to whom I owe a debt of gratitude. Thank you, Phyllis Waters, for always believing in me. A very special thanks to my dear friends Debbie Edmondson, Lucy Allen, and Cynthia Williams, whom I consider my "cupbearers." Their honest opinions and critiques after reading each conversation as well as their continued prayers throughout this endeavor helped me to stay focused and move forward. I am so grateful for my pastor, Robby Stewart, who devoted much of his time to reading the entire curriculum and assuring me that it was biblically sound. My niece, Whitney Smith, and my daughter, Lauren Swinnie, agreed to help pilot this curriculum by using it as a personal Bible study tool. Their reflections were amazing and gave me affirmation that the material flowed together as it was intended. I am extremely grateful for my Sunday school students who helped me pilot this as well. I used this curriculum to teach them each week, and their reflections and critiques were extremely helpful. A very special thank you to Jan Allen for taking my vision for the cover of this book and then creating a masterpiece.

Last but not least, I thank my husband, Jeff, for reading these conversations as well. He really looked forward to receiving them each morning, and when I finally completed the last conversation, he jokingly said, "So, what happened? Did God just stop talking to you?" I assured him that wasn't the case! Jeff keeps me laughing and truly encouraged me throughout the whole process.

Rick Warren said, "We often miss hearing God's voice simply because we aren't paying attention." Maybe it is just that simple! It is my earnest prayer that whoever picks up and dives into this curriculum will indeed pay attention to God's voice and bear fruit for his kingdom.

Kathy M. Crouch

FROM THE MASTER'S HAND TO MINE

Be still and know that I am God,
Is the verse that by design;
Inspired the words on these pages,
From the Master's hand to mine.
If you, like me, have questions,
And know not where to look;
God has so many answers,
Tucked neatly inside of this book.
There is only one requirement,
You must learn to listen well.
God has words of wisdom,
And promises to tell.
He may speak as thunder,
Or whisper into your ear;
But how you choose to listen,
Will determine what you hear.
As you begin this journey,
May God's Spirit lead the way;
To a bright and hopeful future,
As you seek God's voice today.

Kathy M. Crouch

HOW IT WORKS FOR BIBLE STUDY

- Each conversation consists of three parts plus a poem: Let's Get Started, the Conversation, and the Scripture Application. It will be up to your discretion as to how many days to devote to each conversation in its entirety.
- Supplies needed: Bible, pencil, highlighter, journal (optional).
- Begin with *Let's Get Started*. There are Scripture references listed in italics on the page. Locate these, and be ready to read them at the appropriate time. These verses will be embedded inside each conversation.
- Read each question. Answers may be personal reflections or recorded in a journal.
- Now read *A Conversation with God*. (If there is more than one person, alternate voices.)
- Immediately following the reading, write your reflection of the conversation. This should only take two or three minutes. What did it say to you?
- With a highlighter, go back over the conversation, find and highlight the scriptures previously read that are embedded inside.
- Use the scriptures provided to read and possibly commit to memory.
- Complete the Scripture Application.

How It Works for Small Groups

- Each conversation consists of three parts plus a poem: Let's Get Started, the Conversation, and the Scripture

Application. It will be up to your discretion as to how many days to devote to each conversation in its entirety.

- Supplies needed: Bible, pencil, highlighter.
- Begin with *Let's Get Started*. There are Scripture references listed on the page. Before the lesson begins, assign one person per scripture. It should be located in their Bible and ready to read at the appropriate time. These verses will be embedded inside each conversation.
- Read each question aloud to the group. Encourage discussion of each question and use this time to share any experiences you may have had in these areas.
- Now read *A Conversation with God* with your group. One person reads the voice of God. All others alternate to read Kathy's voice.
- Immediately following the reading, have each person write their reflections on the conversation. This should only take two or three minutes. What did it say to them?
- Encourage the group to share their responses to the conversation. Be sensitive as some may not feel comfortable sharing.
- With highlighters, have each person go back over the conversation independently, find and highlight the scriptures previously read that are embedded inside.
- Encourage each person to read the scriptures throughout the week and possibly commit them to memory.
- Complete the Scripture Application.

CHAPTER 1

BE STILL AND KNOW

- Psalm 46:10–11 ESV: *"Be still and know that I am God. I will be exalted among the nations; I will be exalted in the earth! The Lord of hosts is with us; the God of Jacob is our fortress."*
- Isaiah 55:8, 9 ESV: *"For my thoughts are not your thoughts, neither are your ways my ways, declares the Lord. For as the heavens are higher than the earth, so are my ways higher than your ways and my thoughts than your thoughts."*

Let's Get Started

1. Do you have a favorite Bible verse? What makes it so special to you? Are there any verses hanging up or sitting around in your house?
2. Why do you think people display Bible verses in their homes?
3. Do you ever take time out of your day to just sit still in the presence of God? Is it hard for you to sit still? If so, what makes it hard?
4. Are there things going on in our world today that cause you to worry? Do you go to God with your worries? Do

you feel better after you share your concerns with him? Why or why not?

5. Read *Psalm 46: 10, 11*. What do these verses say to you?

6. When you pray, do you pray for God's will to be done in the matter?

7. When you pray, do you feel like your prayers are being answered? Why or why not?

8. Read *Isaiah 55:8, 9*. Would you consider this the "be still" part or the "know" part?

9. Did God speak to you today through the scriptures? If so, how?

A Conversation with God

KATHY. Dear God, I just want to thank you for Psalm 46:10. That is my favorite verse in the Bible.

GOD. *You are welcome, Kathy. Why do you like it so much?*

KATHY. Well, I like the way it sounds—"be still and know that I am God"—I just love that!

GOD. *What have you done with it?*

KATHY. Well, I have at least three Psalm 46:10 signs in my house given to me over the years, and I even painted one and hung it in one of my rooms.

GOD. *Do you know what it means?*

KATHY. Let's see…it means to be still and know that you are God.

GOD. *Tell me about the still part.*

KATHY. Okay, I get up each morning and I get a cup of freshly brewed coffee and I sit by the fire and get really still as I read my devotion and Bible. Is that what you mean God?

GOD. *Do you pray?*

KATHY. God, you know I pray. I talk to you every day!

GOD. *I know. I always hear your prayers, Kathy, especially the ones lately where you have literally begged me to intervene concerning this pandemic, the election, and all of the evil things that are going on right now.*

KATHY. Yes, God, I have been so worried about the condition of our country, and you tell us in your Word that anything we ask according to your will, you will hear us. You tell us you will never leave or forsake us, so yes, I have been seeking your help in these matters.

GOD. *We will get back to the according to my will part later, but for now, tell me what you notice about the condition of the country, and include the things you don't understand.*

KATHY. Lord, I have never seen anything like it. This pandemic has wreaked havoc all over the world, and this recent election was anything but what I would call normal. Justice has died, and there have been riots in so many cities. Churches have had to close because of the virus, and I am just so worried for the future of my children and grandchildren. It's messy down here!

GOD. *Okay, now let's get back to your favorite verse. What about the know part?*

KATHY. What do you mean, God?

GOD. *When you are still, do you know that I am God?*

KATHY. I don't quite understand.

GOD. *Read the rest of the verse.*

KATHY. Okay, it says, "I will be exalted among the heathen, I will be exalted in the earth."

GOD. *Go ahead, read verse 11.*

KATHY. It says, "The Lord of hosts is with us; the God of Jacob is our refuge."

GOD. *Kathy, it is a good thing to be still and meet with me on a regular basis. I delight in that. I want you to remember this. As you increase your "still time" and sit with me, you will get to know me better. Look at all the things you described that cause you to worry. Only I could have blinded the eyes or deafened the ears of justice. Things happened in such a strange way that you must realize I was and am still in total control. I will always be your refuge no matter what happens. Things are going exactly where I want them to go. You must believe that.*

KATHY. Oh my! It is beginning to make perfect sense! Things have been so weird, and there were times when I wondered where you were. And God, I don't remember praying for your will to be done. I'm pretty sure I was praying for my will to be done this whole time.

GOD. *Yes! Always remember, Kathy, my thoughts are not your thoughts and my ways are not your ways. My ways and my thoughts are much higher than yours. That's the know part. When you begin to know that and understand it, then that verse hanging in your house will take on a whole new meaning.*

KATHY. I am speechless right now, God. You have changed everything for me. I will never look at this world as I once did. I will try to increase my "still time" with you and will try to know you in a much deeper way.

GOD. *I am so glad I could help you move forward, Kathy, and now I have one thing to ask of you.*

KATHY. Yes, God, what is it?

GOD. *Share our conversation with someone who might need to be still and know me better.*

KATHY. I will do that, God. I praise you and thank you for everything. Love always, Kathy.

Reflection of Today's Conversation

_____

_____

_____

_____

_____

Scripture Application

- With only a spoken word, God created everything. God spoke from the beginning of time, and he still speaks today. It is up to us, as his children, to find time out of our busy schedules to not only stop moving but quieting our minds in order to hear from him. It is noisy here, and it will take discipline, urgency, and a strong desire to accomplish this goal; but in the end, God will hear from us, we will hear from him, and the blessings from this interaction will be worth it all.

- As we master the art of being still, it is crucial that we realize whom we are approaching with our requests. "Be still and know that I am God." The "know" part is of vital importance. As we approach the throne of God, we must *know* whom we are speaking with and how much weight that carries.

- Solomon had something to say to us about rushing into the presence of God without first being still and realizing just who God is. Read *Ecclesiastes 5:1, 2*. Discuss the message these verses are conveying to us.

- In *Revelation 4*, John finds himself standing in the throne room of heaven. Read this chapter. How does John's vision remind us of God's greatness? Does it help us realize and know whom we are speaking to as we sit still and begin to pray?

- Read *Psalm 117*. God is a God of love and truth. He and he alone deserves our praise.

Wrap It Up

In Kathy's conversation with God, she was expressing her appreciation for a simple Bible verse hanging in her house. By listening to God's voice, she learned so much more about that verse. As we increase our still time with God and understand the holiness of the one we are speaking with, we will begin to understand who God really is and his desire for our life. Our prayer life will grow as we allow the Spirit to lead us. In the end, he will be exalted among the nations, and everyone will know that he is God.

- Discussion
- Closing prayer

Father,

We praise you today for revealing to us through the Scriptures how holy you are. We praise you for your steadfast love for us. As we increase our still time with you and get to know you better, may we hear your voice and grow more in love with you as we talk to you and read your Word.

Amen

Be still and know that I am God.

—Psalm 46:10

Be Still and Know

Be still oh my child and rest in me,
Know that it is I who will rescue thee.
When you realize you're lost in sin and shame,
It is I who will tenderly call you by name.
I am the Lord Your God, the Lord of hosts;
The Father, Son, and Holy Ghost.
I will be exalted in all the earth,
You will see what salvation is really worth.
To surrender it all means the heart must be changed,
It must be cleaned up and then rearranged.
Thoughts that were once so captured by sin,
Will not be allowed to enter in.
As grace through faith once hears your plead,
The God of heaven will meet your need.
Salvation secured, be still and know;
I will never leave you, nor let you go.

Kathy M. Crouch

CHAPTER 2

HEARING GOD'S VOICE

- 2 Corinthians 12:9 ESV: "*And he said unto me, 'My grace is sufficient for you, for my power is made perfect in weakness.'*"
- 2 Timothy 3:16, 17 ESV: "*All scripture is breathed out by God and profitable for teaching, for reproof, for correction and for training in righteousness, that the man of God may be competent, equipped for every good work.*"
- Psalm 119:105 ESV: "*Your word is a lamp to my feet, and a light to my path.*"
- John 10:27 ESV: "*My sheep hear my voice, and I know them, and they follow me.*"
- Isaiah 30:21 ESV: "*And your ears shall hear a word behind you, saying, 'This is the way, walk in it, when you turn to the right or when you turn to the left.'*"
- John 14:26 ESV: "*But the Helper, the Holy Spirit, whom the Father will send in my name, he will teach you all things and bring to your remembrance all that I have said to you.*"

Let's Get Started

1. Has there ever been anything you wanted to accomplish but thought you weren't capable or weren't good enough?
2. What could be some things that make you feel this way?

3. Did you seek advice? Did you ever seek God's will in the matter?
4. Read *2 Corinthians 12:9*. Who can God use to accomplish his work here on earth?
5. Read *2 Timothy 3:16, 17*. Why is it a good idea to read and memorize Scripture?
6. Read *Psalm 119:105*. What do these words mean to you?
7. Can you say that God has ever spoken to you? Have you heard his voice?
8. What are some things that might keep us from hearing the voice of God?
9. Read *John 10:27*. Who is God referring to in this verse? How can this verse bring comfort to us?
10. Read *Isaiah 30:21*. What is the power of this verse?
11. Read *John 14:26*. When we receive Christ as our Savior, who does God send to us, and what is the result?
12. Did we hear God's voice today? How did we hear God's voice? What tools did God provide for us to hear him today?

A Conversation with God

KATHY. Dear God, I would like to begin this conversation by thanking you for blessing me with forty years of teaching Sunday school. These teens have been such a blessing to me. I will never be able to thank you enough for the lives you have touched using me as your vessel. I know you tell us in your Word that your grace is sufficient for us and your strength is made perfect through weakness. You use the least of these to accomplish your will here on this earth, and I consider myself just that—the least of these. It was by your Spirit and mighty hand that I accomplished anything. I am so grateful. I pray that I have never taken away or added anything from your Word as I taught them.

GOD. *Yes, I knew you would teach these children of mine a long time before you did. I have watched you grow along with your students. Teaching my Word is a serious matter. All Scripture is breathed out by me and is profitable for teaching, for reproof, for correction, and for training in righteousness that you may be competent and equipped for every good work. As long as you seek breath from the Holy Spirit as you teach, you will indeed be a good and faithful servant.*

KATHY. I will always try to seek you as I prepare my lessons. "May your words be a lamp unto my feet and a light unto my path." Could we talk a little today about what the Spirit has laid on my mind to teach my students in the days ahead?

GOD. *Of course, we can. I have laid it upon your heart to teach them the importance of hearing my voice and spending more time with me. That is a very good subject. Teens find themselves caught up in life, and it can sometimes be difficult to direct them in the way they should go. They are distracted by numerous things in the world, and it takes loving guidance and discipline to lead them to a life of prayer and Bible reading. How can I assist you in this?*

KATHY. I used our first conversation to introduce them to the fact that your voice is real if we will just take the time to be still and listen. It went really well. I asked them to write down what they understood from our conversation, and I was pleasantly surprised at what they had to say.

GOD. *The students in your class have known me for many years, and they are now at the age where hearing my voice is crucial in making good decisions. Please tell me a few things they had to say.*

KATHY. It helped one of them understand that you know everything that is happening and you remind us that you are in total control. You are doing things for a reason, and we should trust you. Isn't that great, Lord? I was so blessed by this.

GOD. *It sounds like this person was truly open to what I had to say to you in our conversation.*

KATHY. Yes, and another student said that you hear us every day when we pray and you are glad when we talk to you, but you want us to do more. You want us to live out your words and share them with someone in need. You will always do what's best for us even if we can't see it.

GOD. *What insight your students have. I believe they are ready for the next step in hearing my voice. You will find many examples in my Word where men and women heard my voice in a powerful way. Choosing one of those might be a good way to begin.*

KATHY. Yes, there are so many to choose from, and I plan to introduce my students to several of them. One such man was Elijah. His strength was in knowing your voice. When you spoke, he listened, and he acted. I am going to tell them about the time you told him to go tell King Ahab he was doing a lousy job running the country and that if he didn't shape up, you were going to withhold the rain. Elijah didn't have to wonder if it was you speaking to him, did he, God?

GOD. *No, he knew my voice very well, and he responded immediately. It may have been difficult for him at times, but he was faithful. When he heard my voice, he responded.*

KATHY. There is much to teach concerning Elijah, and I just pray that when I have finished, my students will begin to have a better understanding of what it means to hear your voice as Elijah did and be willing to spend time alone with you. It is my prayer that the sound of your voice will be more important to my students than anything this fast-paced world has to offer.

GOD. *As your students begin to hear my voice, they will call to me, and I will answer them. My sheep will hear my voice and I know them and they follow me. Be sure to share this with them. Also, this verse carries much weight: "And your ears shall hear a word behind you, saying, 'This is the way, walk in it, when you turn to the right or when you turn to the left.'" When they become sensitive to my voice, they will hear me even when I whisper.*

KATHY. O God, I really hope I will be able to teach them how to hear your sweet, loving voice.

GOD. *Kathy, the Holy Spirit, whom I will send, will teach you all things and bring to your remembrance all that I have said to you. Do not worry. Be confident. I will give you wisdom and understanding as you lead them. I am already speaking. I will show you how to teach them to listen.*

KATHY. Thank you, God. This is an exciting journey, and may everything I do with my students redound to your glory and your honor. Please watch over us as we spend time in your Word, learning to be still, to listen, and to hear what you have to say. I trust they will have much to say to you in the days ahead. Love, Kathy.

Reflection of Today's Conversation

_____

_____

_____

_____

_____

_____

Scripture Application

- God demonstrated his superiority to all false gods and their prophets. Because Elijah was sensitive to the voice of God and willing to follow his commands, God used Elijah for such a time as this.
- Read *1 Kings 18:18–40.*
- Elijah's triumph at Mt. Carmel seemed like a victory for him. The fire from heaven came down to vindicate God's cause. The people watching responded in faith. The prophets of Baal were slain, and after Elijah prayed a third time, the rains came again. Then things took a sharp turn. Elijah panicked and ran for his life.
- Read *1 Kings 19:1–10.* Discuss these events.
- Read *1 Kings 19: 11–13.* This is the climax of the story. Elijah heard God's voice not through the wind, not through the earthquake, not in the fire, but in a low whisper. It was in that still, small voice. In reverence, Elijah wrapped his face in his cloak and listened as God assured him he was

not alone. God reminded him of the seven thousand faithful followers in Israel.

Wrap It Up

God will always speak to us. It is up to us to be still and listen. Reverend David Bast said it best:

> When God speaks to us, he will tell us something like this: What matters most is obedience, not success. What matters most is how I feel about you, not how you feel about yourself. What matters most is whether I think your life is valuable and useful, not how the world thinks about you. What matters most is how I will reward you, and my reward for faithful service will be giving you more opportunities to serve, so let's get on with it, shall we?

* Discussion
* Closing prayer

Father,

> Thank you for speaking to us. This conversation and Elijah's faithfulness to you help us better understand how much you care for us. Fill us with your spirit, God. Use us in mighty ways to further your kingdom even when we may feel as though we can't. May we learn to be still and spend time with you in the coming days, and as we do, show us how to grow in the knowledge of the Scriptures as you speak to us. May we hear your voice, God, even if it's almost silent.

Amen

My sheep hear my voice, and I know them, and they follow me.

—John 10:27

My Savior's Voice

Teach me Lord to let go
Show me the vanity of worldly things
The joy they bring
Only for a moment
Then gone
Teach me Lord to let you
Take full control of all my ways
All of my desires
All of my hopes
My dreams
Teach me how to pray
Catch me as I fall on my knees
To worship you
To praise you
Then rise
At that moment I will see
With confidence and will know
I have felt your touch
And have heard
Your voice
As I rest in your arms
Hold me with your righteous hand
Whisper in my ear
Yes, I hear you Lord
I hear you
Amen

Kathy M. Crouch

CHAPTER 3

MIRACLES

- John 20:29 ESV: "*Have you believed because you have seen me? Blessed are those who have not seen and yet have believed.*"
- Hebrews 11:6 ESV: "*Without faith it is impossible to please him, for whoever would draw near to God must believe that he exists and that he rewards those who seek him.*"

Let's Get Started

1. What comes to your mind when you hear the word *miracle*?
2. Has anything ever happened in your life or someone else's life that you would consider a miracle?
3. Can you recall any miracles that were recorded in the Scriptures? Try to name at least three of these. What do you think was the greatest of all miracles in the Bible?
4. Read *John 20:18–29*. How does faith play a powerful role in verse 29? Jesus Christ's resurrection was indeed the greatest miracle of all.
5. Have you ever prayed for a miracle? If so, what happened? When you asked God to step in and possibly give you this miracle, was prayer your first or last resort?

6. Read *Hebrews 11:6*. How important is our faith in this verse? What important thing does this verse say we must do to receive God's rewards?

7. Do you believe God performs miracles today? What could be some avenues by which God might show his goodness or maybe even work in a miraculous way in your life?

8. How did these scriptures speak to you today? What did you learn from them?

A Conversation with God

KATHY. Dear God, I have been thinking about miracles lately. Do you still perform miracles today, or are miracles something that were limited to biblical times?

GOD. *Can you tell me about a time where you witnessed an event and considered it to be a miracle?*

KATHY. There are several that come to mind, but finding a diamond ring in the Atlantic Ocean is at the top of my list. I know you remember that time my niece dropped her ring in the ocean. She was devastated and in tears, and after we all tried our best to reach down into the wet sand to retrieve it, we decided to commit it to you, and the whole family proceeded with prayer.

GOD. *Yes, I remember quite well. Prayer is often the last resort.*

KATHY. I know, Lord. That should have been our first response for sure. The older I get, the more that fact rings true.

GOD. *I heard the prayers loud and clear, so I sent a person to the very place where the ring was dropped. Do you remember who that was and what he did?*

KATHY. Yes, it was my son Lane. He dropped stones in the water in the location where the ring was dropped. We had no idea what he was doing, but later on, we understood that he was trying to figure out if the current would take the stones away. We all prayed as he continued to drop the stones, then we heard him say to my other niece, "It should be right here."

GOD. *If you want to believe in miracles, Kathy, a miracle occurred that day because I stepped into your world to act in response to the prayers. I am a sovereign God, and nothing or no one will ever minimize my ability to act in miraculous ways. Sometimes I work through people. That day, I chose Lane. I knew he had the knowledge and skills to figure out where the ring would be.*

KATHY. Lord, when my niece reached her hand down into the sand that one and only time, she screamed with every ounce of breath she had in her: "I found it!" It was you who found it, right? That was the miracle.

GOD. *Kathy, many people only associate miracles with events that happened in the Bible: crossing the sea on dry land, healing the sick, casting out evil spirits, walking on water, or feeding a multitude with five small loaves of bread and a couple of fish. These were clearly caused by me, not just something that was unusual.*

KATHY. Yes, God, I have heard about those miracles for much of my life. I feel like the attention of those miracles focused entirely on you. Was that your purpose for using them?

GOD. *Well, with Jesus, the miracles were intended to prove that Jesus was from me. This is actually how I established my church. My greatest miracle of all, however, was when my son rose on the third day after the crucifixion. One of the disciples doubted that it happened.*

KATHY. Yes, it was Thomas. I have never fully understood his unbelief.

GOD. *Thomas, like many people today, had to see the nail marks and put his finger where the nails were in order to believe. Jesus said to him, "Have you believed because you have seen me? Blessed are those who have not seen and yet have believed." What I need for you to understand, Kathy, is that when you see things happen that you can't explain or you feel that after a season of sincere prayer your prayer was indeed answered, it was by faith that you believed and not by sight. Whom you give the glory to after—that is what really matters.*

KATHY. So are you saying that what happened that day at the ocean could be considered a miracle because as we prayed, we had faith and believed that the ring would be found? We knew that finding a small diamond ring in the Atlantic Ocean was totally out of our control and only someone much greater than any of us could find it?

GOD. *Wait a minute. It was not* we *had faith, not* we *believed but* someone.

KATHY. Oh, that stings and really puts things into perspective.

GOD. *Kathy, all who believe are blessed, but even more, those who believe apart from a ring being found in the depths of the ocean. Faith is a powerful thing, and without it, it will be impossible to please me. For whoever would draw near to me must believe that I exist and that I reward those who seek me. Faith is everything.*

KATHY. So someone had that kind of faith that day, right, Lord? They were diligent in seeking you? Whoever it was truly felt in their heart that the only way that ring was going to be recovered was through divine intervention?

GOD. *Exactly.*

KATHY. That is so awesome, God. It is very clear to me now. Thank you for helping us find that ring. Thank you for that person who had the kind of faith needed at that very moment. I sincerely hope that you were clearly seen by everyone there in all that happened that day. As for me, I pray that my faith will grow from day to day, hour by hour, minute by minute to be like the person who prayed that day who had enough faith to believe in something that could not be seen. I love you, Lord, and thanks for everything you do for us here on this earth while we wait for your return. Love, Kathy.

Reflection of Today's Conversation

_____

_____

_____

_____

_____

_____

Scripture Application

- A miracle of God is an extraordinary event that reveals God's power. Jesus performed numerous miracles. He had many reasons for doing so, but the main reason was to prove that he was who he said he was. He was indeed the son of God.

- John in John 20:30, 31 said, "Now Jesus did many other signs in the presence of the disciples, which are not written in the book. But these are written so that you may believe that Jesus is the Christ, the son of God, and that by believing you may have life in his name." John 21:25 says, "Now there are also many other things that Jesus did. Were every one of them to be written, I suppose that the world itself could not contain the books that would be written." Wow! That is a lot of miracles.

- Three famous miracles are recorded in the Old Testament. God's creation is recorded in Genesis 1–2, God using Moses to part the Red Sea is recorded in Exodus 14:21–22, and the sun and moon standing still is recorded in Joshua 10:12–14.

- Only three miracles recorded appear in all four gospels: his own resurrection (Matthew 28, Mark 16, Luke 24, and John 20), the feeding of the five thousand (Matthew 14:13–21, Mark 6:30–44, Luke 9:10–17, and John 6:1–14), Jesus healing the blind (Matthew 9:27–31, Mark 8:22–26, Luke 18:35–43, and John 9).

- I encourage you to take time to read all of these scriptures and think about the many miracles of God.

- What miracles were recorded in these scriptures?
  - Matthew 14:25–27: _____
  - Daniel 6:21–22: _____
  - Daniel 3:25: _____
  - Matthew 8:23–27: _____

Wrap It Up

These are just a few of the miracles found in the Scriptures. There are many more to be discovered. The conversation Kathy had with God showed her that sometimes he will place people in our path to be used by him to show us great things that only he could control—like finding a ring in the ocean. One of the greatest miracles of all is when God takes a sinner, forgives his sins, adopts him as his child, and grants him everlasting life. Praise the Lord for the free gift of salvation. It truly is a miracle.

- Discussion
- Closing prayer

Father,

We thank you today for revealing to us how powerful you are through the many miracles you performed all through the Scriptures. Most of all, thank you for the miracle of your resurrection; and because you live, we can receive the miracle of salvation. May we always remember that you are a God of power and glory. Give us the strength to follow you all the days of our lives.

Amen

Have you believed because you have seen me? Blessed are those who have not seen and yet have believed.

—John 20:29

Miracles

Do you believe in miracles?
Does your faith take you that far?
Can the one who walked on the water,
Still move right where you are?
The key to unlocking the miracle door,
Can be found in the place where you start.
For Jesus could not do one miracle,
Without the Spirit of God in his heart.
Is your heart filled with God's Holy Spirit?
Does he dwell in that secret place?
When you lift up your voice to praise him,
Do you meet with him face to face?
That one simple step will open the door,
And the miracles will be set free.
Once the power of the Spirit takes over your life,
The first miracle you will then clearly see.
The miracle of life everlasting,
Yes, the miracle of forgiveness of sins.
The miracle of God's Holy Spirit,
The miracle where true life begins.
Do you believe in miracles?
Does your faith really take you that far?
Will the One who died to save you,
Be invited to live where you are?

Kathy M. Crouch

CHAPTER 4

CHILDLIKE FAITH

- Matthew 18:3 ESV: "*Truly I say to you, unless you turn and become like little children, you will never enter the kingdom of heaven.*"
- Luke 9:23 ESV: "*If anyone would come after me, let him deny himself and take up his cross daily and follow me.*"
- John 3:3 ESV: "Jesus answered him, '*Truly truly I say unto you, unless one is born again, he cannot see the kingdom of God.*'"
- Ephesians 2:8 ESV: "*For by grace you have been saved through faith, and this is not your own doing, it is a gift of God.*"

Let's Get Started

1. Read *Matthew 18:3*. What does this scripture say to you? Make a list of characteristics a two- or three-year-old child possesses.
2. Do you still possess any of these characteristics? If so, which ones; and if not, why not?
3. What or whom do little children tend to put their faith in? What can take away our childlike faith as we grow up?
4. Read *Luke 9:23*. Who was Jesus talking to? Why is it difficult to deny ourselves in order to follow Jesus?

5. Read *John 3:3*. What must we do to see the kingdom of God? Can we begin to see God's kingdom here on earth once we are saved? What makes that possible?
6. Read *Ephesians 2:8*. What is the key word here? Have you ever thought of salvation as a gift? Is there anything we can do to earn it?
7. What do you hope to learn in today's conversation?

A Conversation with God

KATHY. Dear God, I was reading a story the other day about a thirty-year-old man who is mentally disabled as a result of difficulties during labor. He has the mind of a seven-year-old. His name is Kevin, and he believes that you live under his bed. Do you know who I am talking about?

GOD. *Yes, Kevin is very special. Although he functions as a child, he has had a good life with parents and a sister who love him dearly.*

KATHY. As I was reading the story, I thought about Matthew 18:3, which says, "Truly I tell you, unless you change and become like little children, you will never enter the kingdom of heaven." I know you were addressing your disciples here, but doesn't that also apply to us?

GOD. *When the disciples asked me the question "Who then is the greatest in the kingdom of heaven," I had to let them know that there is no scorekeeping in heaven. I consistently pointed to children as an example of how to become citizens of my kingdom. Childlike faith is a virtue—oh, that more people could possess such a thing.*

KATHY. The story went on to say that Kevin doesn't know anything exists outside of his world. He doesn't know what it means to be discontent. His life is simple. He will never know the entanglement of wealth or power. He doesn't care what kind of clothes he wears and recognizes no differences in people. His needs are always met, and he never worries that one day they may not be. Lord, I do not know any adult that fits that description—especially me.

GOD. *Yes, Kevin's heart is pure. He still believes everyone tells the truth, promises must be kept, and he is not afraid to cry when he is hurt, angry, or sorry. He trusts me completely. That is why he thinks I live under his bed. I guess in a way, I do.*

KATHY. Lord, I have so much to learn from this. I mean, as I continue to grow and am a part of this world, the things that Kevin experiences on a daily basis I lost a very long time ago. How can I get back to that place because I really want to enter heaven one day.

GOD. *The disciples were with my son, but they had not entered the kingdom, and they would not until they changed. They had to receive the Holy Spirit for any of this to make sense. Jesus told Nicodemus that unless he was born again, he could not enter the kingdom of God. This just meant that being regenerated comes with this childlikeness. To become like children, we need to be like Kevin, who is humble and totally dependent on his earthly father. You must be willing to deny yourself, pick up your cross, follow me, and trust me with everything.*

KATHY. As the story came to an end, it said that Kevin really seemed to know you and was your friend. You are his closest companion, aren't you God?

GOD. *Yes, this is a very hard concept for adults to understand because Kevin is not confined by intellectual reasoning. He comes to me as a child. This is not as hard as it seems. If I tell you that you must become as a child to enter my kingdom, do you think I would make it impossible for you to achieve it?*

KATHY. Well, of course not, Lord, but I have a long way to go. I am so glad I read this story. Kevin has taught me many things. When he goes to bed at night, he says, "Are you there, God? Where are you? Oh, I see. Under the bed."

GOD. *Yes, he cannot see me, but he knows I am there. Not a single night goes by that Kevin doesn't make sure I am under his bed. I never disappoint him!*

KATHY. I am so thankful that I have been saved by grace through faith and it is not of my own doing; it is a gift from you, God. Now, with your help, I will try to acquire some of those wonderful traits that Kevin never had to learn. I really enjoyed our conversation today, Lord. Love, Kathy.

Reference: *Stories for a teens Heart* compiled by Alice Gray, Multnomah Publishers, Inc. 1999

Reflection of Today's Conversation

———————————————————————
———————————————————————
———————————————————————
———————————————————————
———————————————————————
———————————————————————

Scripture Application

- Review Hebrews 11:1: "Faith means being sure of the things we hope for and knowing that something is real even if we do not see it."
- Hebrews 11:6: "Without faith no one can please God. Anyone who comes to God must believe that he is real and rewards those who truly want to find him."
- This kind of faith was exhibited in the Old Testament. Many heroes provided examples of faith and obedience to God. Faith is the reason we remember great people who lived in the past.
- Read *Hebrews 11: 8–17*. Discuss the great faith that Abraham displayed in these scriptures.
- Read *Hebrews 11: 23–28*. How did the faith of Moses show how deeply devoted he was to God?
- Read *Hebrews 11:29, 30*. Who showed great faith in these verses?
- Read *James 2:14–24*. Having faith is important, but discuss the importance of putting our faith into action. Faith with no effort is no faith at all. People are made right with God by what they do, not by faith only.

Wrap It Up

Max Lucado summed up the eleventh chapter of Hebrews like this:

> Faith is more than a belief in God. It is also
> a way of life. Heroes of faith, although imperfect,
> trusted God and gave their lives to him.

He also went on to say, "Faith is the belief that God is real and that God is good." This is much like the belief that Kevin had in the confinements of his world. He believed that all was good, and he trusted that God was real and lived under his bed. What can you do today to demonstrate your faith? How can you become like one of these heroes or maybe even a Kevin?

- Discussion
- Closing prayer

Father in heaven,

> We humbly come before you today, confessing that we have a long way to go in learning what Kevin never had to learn. Having the faith of a child is simply putting all of our trust in you and believing that no matter what we may face in our day-to-day experiences, you are in control and will lead us every step of the way. Thank you for revealing this truth to us, and please guide us as we begin this journey together with you.

Amen

Jesus said, "Truly I tell you, unless you change and become like little children, you will never enter the kingdom of heaven."

—Matthew 18:3

Childlike Faith

Childlike faith is a virtue, difficult to achieve once you're grown.
A two-year-old child is totally dependent upon someone.
His heart is pure and nothing exists outside of his world.
His life is simple and he knows nothing of wealth.
His clothes need not match.
His needs are always met.
He never has to worry that one day they may not be.
Everyone tells the truth. Promises must
be kept. He trusts completely.
Oh God in heaven,
The scripture is clear.
As we grow older, the world has a way of
lessening our dependence on you.
To Become like little children again seems impossible to many of us.
But you are a God of love.
You would never require a thing we could not achieve.
Like,
Obtaining what a two-year-old never has to learn.
Understanding, apart from you, we are powerless
over the circumstances of our lives.
Seeing your Kingdom here on this earth through
your glorious eyes, only possible by the
leading of your Spirit.
Reaching the level of humility needed to show
how dependent we are upon you.
Open our eyes and humble us, Lord.
Pour out your spirit and cover us with mercy and grace.
Teach us to trust you with everything.
Teach us how to have the faith of a child.
We need to learn again.
May we trust, love, and totally depend on you.
Take our hand.

Lead us as we take up our cross and follow you everywhere you go,
and then…on our final day,
May we be found skipping down that very narrow path;
to your Kingdom,
in heaven.
Amen

Kathy M. Crouch

CHAPTER 5

A PRIDEFUL HEART

- Jeremiah 17:9 ESV: *"The human heart is deceitful above all things, and desperately wicked; who can understand it?"*
- Proverbs 16:5 ESV: *"Anyone who is arrogant in heart is an abomination to me and be assured, it will not go unpunished."*
- James 4:6 ESV: *"God opposes the proud, but give grace to the humble."*
- Proverbs 29:23 ESV: *"One's pride will bring him low, but he who is lowly in spirit will obtain honor."*

Let's Get Started

1. Webster defines *pride* as *"the quality or state of being proud: such as inordinate self-esteem: Conceit; delight or elation arising from some act, possession, or relationship."* What comes to your mind when you hear the word *pride*?
2. Read *James 4:6*. What seems to be the opposite of pride in this verse? God opposes one and gives grace to the other. What are your thoughts? What do you think about when you hear the word *humble*? Webster defines it as *"not proud or haughty: not arrogant or assertive."*

3. In today's conversation, God helps Kathy understand that when pride takes up residence in one's heart, it can keep that person from seeking him. Why do you think that is?

4. Read *Jeremiah 17:9*. How does God view the human heart? What do we as Christians know is the only thing that can cleanse our hearts of all unrighteousness? (1 John 1:9)

5. God says having a prideful heart is a sin. Pride, if left unattended, can kill, steal, and destroy. What can we do, as God's children, if we feel like there may be signs of pride in ourselves or in someone else close to us? Read *Proverbs 29:23*. What must we pray for?

6. Read *Proverbs 16:5*. That warning should open our eyes as to the seriousness of allowing pride to take over our hearts. What are your thoughts concerning this verse? Psalm 51:10 says, "Create in me a clean heart, oh God, and renew a right spirit within me." The psalmist knew the meaning of a prideful heart.

A Conversation with God

KATHY. Dear God, our country is going in the wrong direction. It has been spiraling out of control for a very long time, but it seems as though it is about to crash. I am carrying a heavier burden right now for those who are lost and do not know you as their Savior. They don't even know they don't know. That's the hard part for me. Lord, what is the one thing inside of a lost man's heart that is difficult to soften and change?

GOD. *I am so glad you asked this question. The answer might surprise you because it is something that many people suffer from and do not even recognize it. The answer is pride. If pride has taken up residence in one's heart, apart from me, it is nearly impossible to remove. Pride is a sin, and if one does not realize they possess this, it will infect many decisions they make.*

KATHY. What are some red flags, so to speak, to look for?

GOD. *A proud man will say he does not need me. Pride has its roots in a feeling of wealth and accomplishments which is then used to com-*

pare. He thinks of himself as higher than someone else. He is arrogant, and all of these things come from deep inside of his heart. The human heart is deceitful above all things and desperately wicked; who can understand it? Anyone who is arrogant in heart is an abomination to me, and be assured, it will not go unpunished.

KATHY. That is why this is weighing so heavily on my heart. So, is it wrong to be proud of an achievement? Is this the pride you are talking about? There have been many times that I have been proud of my children for things they have been able to achieve.

GOD. *There is a difference. As long as you understand that whatever was achieved was a direct moving of my hand and you acknowledge that, it is good. The problem arises when one begins to delight less in the praise and more in themselves. Sinful pride is giving yourselves credit for something that I have accomplished. The kind of pride that stems from self-righteousness or conceit is sin, and it is a hindrance to keep someone from seeking me.*

KATHY. C. S. Lewis said something that really spoke to me. He said, "As long as you are proud, you cannot know God. A proud man is always looking down on things and people and, of course, as long as you are looking down, you cannot see something that is above you." Could that something above that he is talking about be you God?

GOD. *Yes, Kathy. Those who do not think they are sick will never seek a doctor. Those who do not know they are lost will not seek a Savior. They will never look up on their own. Pride can kill, steal, and destroy.*

KATHY. Please help me know what to do with this burden I am carrying. Help me to discern if those I am praying for are suffering from pride. Please tell me how to pray for them.

GOD. *When I give you a burden, I place on your heart a compassion for a person or a need. My Spirit will always guide you as to what and how you should pray. Be sensitive to my voice. If you have someone in mind who possesses any of the things I have described, you may want to pray for humility to take up residence in that person's heart. A humble heart will set things in proper order and perspective.*

Only when the heart is clothed in humility can it see things clearly. Always remember, I oppose the proud but give grace to the humble.

KATHY. Lord, as I said at the beginning of our conversation, I fear that much of this world has abandoned you and I feel that you have had about enough of our arrogance and I am sure that at times, you are so disappointed in your creation. Forgive me where I fall short in serving you as I should. Thank you for laying the burden upon my shoulders to pray for those who need you so desperately. What an honor and privilege it is.

GOD. *Your faithfulness will not go unnoticed, and I promise to hear you when you pray. Pride is a hard thing to break. Remember, it was Satan who helped motivate Adam and Eve in the garden to become greater than what I had created them to be. It was not in them as I created them, but it entered into their thinking in Satan's presence. Pride has been in the world for a very long time. It saddens me to know that many people will never realize the potential that awaits them if they would just let go of their pride and move forward in my plan.*

KATHY. It saddens me as well, Lord. Thank you for our talk today. Rick Warren said, "True humility is not thinking less of yourself; it is thinking of yourself less." What powerful words! That one action could solve many things, couldn't it, God?

GOD. *Yes, indeed! The opposite of pride is humility. One's pride will bring him low, but he who is lowly in spirit will obtain honor.*

KATHY. Thank you for imparting much wisdom unto me today, Lord. You really cleared things up for me. Love, Kathy.

Reflection of Today's Conversation

_____

_____

_____

_____

_____

_____

Scripture Application

- Pride is dangerous because it convinces us that our gifts and abilities come from ourselves instead of from God. Pride causes us, through our wealth and accomplishments, to compare. It can cause us to boast and think very highly of ourselves. Read *Proverbs 16:18, 19.* The nature of pride, self-will, and arrogance is destructive, and a haughty spirit will cause us to fall.
- Satan was God's most beautiful angel. Not being content with that position, he rebelled by becoming prideful, full of envy, and he wanted to be God. Satan fell because of pride. Read *Isaiah 14: 12–15.*
- Read *Ezekiel 28 13–19.* Most Bible interpreters believe that these verses compare the pride of the king of Tyre to the pride of Satan. Both wanted to be God. Verse 16 is speaking directly to Lucifer but is also speaking to the king of Tyre. This king is a type of Satan. Just as God cast Satan out of heaven due to his pride, God will cast the king of Tyre off his throne as well. Just as Satan elevated himself because of his pride, the king of Tyre had been elevated up by the people. Now he is brought down in front of those people and will be no more. God will destroy him. Satan's final destiny also awaits him as indicated in Revelation 20:10: "And the devil who had deceived them was thrown into the lake of fire and sulfur where the beast and the false prophets were, and they will be tormented day and night forever and ever."
- Satan was then, and is still today, influencing kings. A good modern-day example of this is Iran, a country in Western Asia with its leader Ali Khamenei. The goal of this boastful and prideful leader is to annihilate the Jewish people. Khamenei is as Prince of Tyre. The same demonic forces that were working during the reign of Satan are working behind the scenes today as he was in our scripture.
- Read *Genesis 3:1–6.* It was Satan who helped motivate Adam and Eve to think they could be greater than what God created them to be.

- Read *Genesis 3:14, 15* to see God's judgment against Satan for tempting Adam and Eve.
- Read *Revelation 20:10*. What will be Satan's ultimate punishment?

Wrap It Up

The same demonic forces we read about are still in our world today. Pride is still at work in the lives of many people. The kind of pride that stems from self-righteousness is a sin, and it will keep us from seeking God. Understanding that we can do nothing apart from God and that in our own strength we can do nothing to inherit eternal life is essential to becoming a follower of Christ. It is pride that causes people to stumble and never realize these truths. Andrew Murray said, "Pride must die in you, or nothing in heaven can live in you." Let us meditate on these words today and search our hearts to see if there is any hidden pride to be found.

- Discussion
- Closing prayer

Father,

> You are our refuge and strength, a very present help in trouble. You hate pride, so if there is an ounce of pride living within us, help us realize it and then deliver us from it. May the Holy Spirit shine his light upon us so that we may see if there is any pride hiding in the secret places of our hearts. Open our eyes from this day forward so that we may see clearly and know when pride has slipped in. Please help us to become the humble servants you've called us to be.

Amen

One's pride will bring him low, but he who is
lowly in spirit will obtain honor.

—Proverbs 29:23

A Prideful Heart

Humble said to Pride, hey, what's up with all this greed?
Pride said to Humble, well I have everything I need.
Accomplishments are great and arrogance is there,
Without these, I'd be lost because I use them to compare.
Pride said to humble, hey, why do you seem so weak?
Humble said to Pride, well I am lowly and I am meek.
Compassion fills my heart along with gentle love and care,
Jesus is my mentor and I take him everywhere.
Those traits are the opposite of all that I possess,
That doesn't mean that Jesus would ever love me less.
But Pride, you do not understand you have a wicked heart,
God knew your bad intentions; he knew them from the start.
You showed up in the garden with Adam and Eve,
Your greatest work was done that day and that was to deceive.
You told them they were greater than God wanted them to be,
Sin may not have entered in had you acted more like me.
Humble said to Pride, well I guess you're here to stay,
It saddens me to think that it just has to be this way.
Please listen very carefully, I need for you to know,
A humble spirit obtains honor, a man's pride will bring him low.

Kathy M. Crouch

CHAPTER 6

TAKING THE PEN AWAY

- Psalm 46:10 ESV: *"Be still and know that I am God."*
- Revelation 22:13 ESV: *"I am the alpha and the omega, the first and the last, the beginning and the end."*
- Jeremiah 29:13 ESV: *"When you seek me, you will find me, when you search me with all of your heart."*
- 2 Timothy 3:16, 17 ESV: *"All scripture is breathed out by God and profitable for teaching, for reproof, for correction, and for training in righteousness, that the man of God might be complete, equipped for every good work."*
- James 4:8 ESV: *"Draw near to God and he will draw near to you."*
- 1 John 2:16 ESV: *"For all that is in the world, the desires of the flesh and the desires of the eyes and pride of life is not from the Father, but is from the world."*
- Psalm 51:10 ESV: *"Create in me a clean heart and renew a right spirit within me."*

Let's Get Started

1. Read *Psalm 46:10*. In the very first conversation, Kathy talked about being still and hearing God's voice. In today's

conversation, she had to revisit that same conversation. Why do you think that happened?

2. Do you think God means we must sit completely still in one place in order to hear from him? Why or why not? Do you think we can hear from God through the noise?

3. What tends to keep us from hearing the voice of God?

4. Read *Revelation 22:13*. How does this verse help us to remember that God is the one true God? Do you agree that understanding how holy God is and how much weight that carries helps us with the "know" part?

5. Read *Jeremiah 29:13*. On a scale of 1–10, how diligent have you been in searching for God and actually feeling as though you found him? What is the difference between knowing and hearing? Give an example.

6. Read *2 Timothy 3:16*. What is Scripture profitable for? Read *James 4:8*. What is the result of digging into the Scriptures?

7. Read *1 John 2:16*. What are these worldly things that often keep us from growing closer to God?

8. Read *Psalm 51:10*. How do you think this conversation might end if Kathy takes all of these scriptures to heart and applies them to her life?

A Conversation with God

KATHY. Dear God, it has been several days since we have talked. I have found it difficult to write or get my thoughts together. Today, however, I was doing yard work, and I heard you speak again.

GOD. *I had to take away your pen. Remember this day because it is a very special day. I had to take you to the very place where our first conversation began. You needed to start over with that very same verse, "Be still and know that I am God."*

KATHY. What do you mean? You know that is my favorite verse. We talked a lot about it in our first conversation.

GOD. *Kathy, you may somewhat understand the know part of that verse, but I see who will be reading these, so let's revisit it for a moment.*

Being still doesn't necessarily mean sitting on your couch without moving. I had to send you back to the yard. When you were there, were you moving? Was there noise all around you?

KATHY. Yes, Lord. I was definitely moving and the birds were singing extra loudly and I even thought about how loud the road noise was today.

GOD. *But you heard me through the noise. You were focused, and you talked to me just like you did in our first conversation. You can be busy and still hear my voice. It was easy for you today. But do you remember the one important thing I told you?*

KATHY. You said it was not about me. It is about you. That brings to mind one of my most cherished quotes. Max Lucado said, "God does not exist to make a big deal out of us. We exist to make a big deal out of him. It's not about you. It's not about me. It's about him." It's about you, God—you and only you!

GOD. *Yes, it is all about me. Anyone who reads our conversations must know that I am the one true God. I am the supreme creator of all. I am holy; I am the alpha and the omega, the first and the last, the beginning and the end. I redeem the lost, pardon iniquities, heal broken hearts, love, satisfy, renew, strengthen, and I give eternal life. The "know" part in that verse that you love so much carries much weight. It must not be taken lightly or forgotten.*

KATHY. I know and believe all of those things, God. I have just had a hard time hearing you lately. I honestly think that in some of our conversations, I have been doing most of the talking and haven't been listening as I should. Today, when I was alone and doing yard work, I could hear you clearly. It was as if you are working right along beside me. You said so much. Does this mean I have to get all dirty and pull weeds for our conversations to continue?

GOD. *No, but what made the difference? What caused the silence before today? What kept you from seeking me and hearing my voice in other places?*

KATHY. I must confess that I've been busy. That always gets in the way, and I'm pretty good at it.

GOD. *It takes discipline to spend time with me, and for some, it may be difficult at times to learn what my voice sounds like. Reading my Word and spending time in prayer will bring my voice to life. I may speak loudly, or I may whisper; but when it is heard, big things happen. When you seek me, you will find me when you search me with all of your heart. The Bible is filled with people who did incredible things because they knew my voice, searched me, found me, and spent time with me.*

KATHY. I feel confident that I know your voice, God, even though I will never know everything about you on this side of heaven.

GOD. *Yes, that is true, but the things of this world can get in the way and keep you from seeking me and from hearing my voice. There is a huge difference between knowing and hearing. You must listen. You got distracted over the past few days, that's all.*

KATHY. Lord, thank you for turning me around. Thank you for taking the pen away. The "know" part in that verse is so important because when we know whom we are setting our time aside for and know who you really are, it will make all the difference in how we structure our day.

GOD. *That is exactly right. Remember, there are lessons to be learned as you read my Word. All scripture is breathed out by me and profitable for teaching, for reproof, for correction, and for training in righteousness that the man of God might be complete, equipped for every good work. Make sure you spend time there. When you know these things about me, you will draw near to me, and I promise to draw near to you. One more important thing I leave with you: For all that is in the world, the desires of the flesh and the desires of the eyes and pride of possessions is not from me but is from the world. Now again, I give you the* pen. *Use it wisely. Be ever so still, and know that I am God.*

KATHY. Yes, Lord. My heart is full. Please forgive me where I have failed you. I ask that you create in me a clean heart and renew a right spirit within me. Slow me down, remove the distractions, and may I never again let the things of this world come before you. Love, Kathy.

Reflection of Today's Conversation

_____

_____

_____

_____

_____

_____

Scripture Application

- In this conversation, Kathy revealed the fact that she was struggling to converse with God. She wasn't hearing his voice as clearly as before. God took her back to the very first conversation to remind her of the importance of being still in his presence and knowing to whom she is communicating with. It was the distractions in her life that were clearly getting in the way. She realized that being still was not ceasing to move; it was simply setting aside the time to focus her attention solely on the Lord. She understood that he still speaks to her through the background noises. It was the business that kept her from hearing him.

- The definition of _distraction_ is "anything that prevents someone from giving full attention to something else." Satan uses distractions to keep us busy. Sometimes he even uses worry, fear, and anxiety for that same purpose. John 10:10 says, "The thief comes to kill, steal, and destroy." A stern warning comes from 1 Peter 5:8: "Be sober-minded; be watchful. Your adversary the devil prowls around like a roaring lion, seeking someone to devour." These verses clearly show us how easily Satan can draw us away from conversing with God if we let our guard down.

- Today we will look in the Scriptures to see how a certain individual struggled with this same affliction. Read _Luke 10:38–42._

- Our attention is usually focused on what is important to us. Distractions can and will reveal what we love. This is what happened to Martha. Think about this. When you are preparing for guests to come dine around your table, chances are you are concentrating on making sure your house is clean, your table looks inviting, you've prepared enough food, etc. Martha could only complain that Mary wasn't helping her with all of the tiny details it takes to impress others. All of Martha's business took her eyes off the most important thing of the evening—Jesus! It was then that Jesus had to remind Martha of this truth. Mary, sitting at the feet of Jesus, was indeed what mattered most that evening.

Wrap It Up

Luke 12:34 reminds us, "For where your treasure is, there will your heart be also." Staying connected to God is vitally important, but it takes a daily commitment and discipline to keep God first. Daily distractions get in our way, and then spending time with God becomes last on our list of things to do. James 4:8 tells us to "Draw near to God and he will draw near to you." No matter how far you seem to drift from God, the good news is that he will call you back into that close relationship with him. All that's required on your part is to "be still and know that he is God."

- Discussion
- Closing prayer

Father,

We humbly come before you right now, asking for your forgiveness for the times we have let the things of this world lure us away from you. Fill us with the desire to seek after you each and every day. Crush every distraction that Satan may put in our path, and fill our hearts with your spirit so that we may hear your still small voice even through the noise.

Amen

For all that is in the world, the desires of the flesh and the desires of the eyes and pride of life is not from the father, but is from the world.

—1 John 2:16

Taking the Pen Away

The words just would not come to me,
As I began to write today.
Could you please tell me, dear God above,
Why you took the pen away?
*I am always there to guide your hand,
And to watch the joy it brings.
But Satan has you distracted now,
And focused on lesser things.*
Like cleaning, cooking, and shopping for things,
Just to name a few?
Is that how Satan distracts me, Lord,
And keeps me away from you?
*Yes, indeed he's a crafty deceiver,
So, it doesn't take him long;
To steal the time set aside for me,
And to remove you from where you belong.*
At times I get so discouraged,
And I know it's the devil's ploy;
To fill my day with worldly things,
And to take away my joy.
From the Master's hand to mine,
Flow the words I have lost today.
I see that taking the pen from me,

Was really the only way.
I had to feel the emptiness,
And realize the miles I'd drifted.
It only took a moment,
To lose what I was gifted.
Forgive me, Lord, I humbly pray,
For the worldly things I do.
With pen in hand, may I hear your voice,
As I find my way back to you.

Kathy M. Crouch

CHAPTER 7

RAINY DAYS

- Isaiah 41:10 ESV: "*Fear not, for I am with you; be not dismayed, for I am your God; I will strengthen you, I will help you. I will uphold you with my righteous right hand.*"
- Psalm 71:5 ESV: "*For thou art my hope. O Lord God; thou art my trust from my youth.*"
- James 1:2, 3 ESV: "*Consider it all joy when you meet trails of various kinds, for you know that the testing of your faith produces steadfastness.*"
- Isaiah 30:21 ESV: "*And your ears shall hear a word behind you, saying, this is the way, walk in it, when you turn to the right or when you turn to the left.*"
- Deuteronomy 31:8 ESV: "*It is I who goes before you. I will be with you; I will not leave you or forsake you. Do not fear or be dismayed.*"

Let's Get Started

1. In today's conversation, Kathy talks about a rainy season she went through at a very young age after the death of her mom. Have you ever lost someone dear to you and found yourself in what Kathy describes as a rainy season?

What emotions or feelings might be associated with a rainy season?

2. God tells us that there are seasons in life that we will go through: "To everything there is a season, and a time to every purpose under heaven." Do you feel as though you are in a particular season right now? What words might describe the various seasons of life?

3. There are many Scripture references where God assures us that he will be with us through these difficult seasons. Let's dive into some of these scriptures and reflect on God's promises.

4. Read *Isaiah 41:10*. Reflection:

_____

_____

5. Read *Psalm 71:5*. Reflection:

_____

_____

6. Read *James: 1:2, 3*. Reflection:

_____

_____

7. Read *Isaiah 30:21*. Reflection:

_____

_____

8. Read *Deuteronomy 31:8*. Reflection:

_____

_____

A Conversation with God

KATHY. Dear God, good morning. Yes, it's raining again, but you have clearly shown me that one day I will thank you for the rain. This sort of leads me into what I want to talk to you about today. There are rainy seasons for our grass, flowers, and crops, but there are rainy days in life. Some days the clouds of life can come over us, and it seems as though the sun will never shine again.

GOD. I *hear you, Kathy, but I will need a little more information.*

KATHY. You called my mother home when I was only sixteen years old. That was a very rainy season for me. I was in high school, trying to find my way, and a girl always needs her mother to help guide her along the way. It was just me and my dad, and although he provided me with all of the essentials of life, he was not there for me as I began to sort out and plan my future. It was just you and me, God. It was just you and me.

GOD. *Kathy, you may never understand any of this until you meet me face to face, but I just want you to know that your mom was sick and very tired. She was ready to get rid of that earthly body and rest in my arms. Your dad is here as well.*

KATHY. My heart rejoices in that truth, God. Although they are there with you, death often leaves a hole right in the middle of one's heart especially when it is a parent or family member that is suddenly taken away. But how did I do it? There were so many decisions to make during that time like graduation, applying to college, taking care of my dad, holding down a job—just life in general.

GOD. *You were much stronger than you knew. I was with you every step of the way. My word says in Isaiah 41:10, "Fear not, for I am with you; be not dismayed, for I am your God; I will strengthen you, I will help you. I will uphold you with my righteous right hand." I helped you make decisions, and I carried you when times got tough. You were never alone in your grief.*

KATHY. I was reading Psalm 71:5 which says, "For thou art my hope. O Lord God; thou art my trust from my youth." That verse rings so loudly in my ear. I was so young, and I could have made so many wrong turns. When I look back on all of it, I clearly see that it was you who took my hand and guided me along the way.

GOD. *Yes, I did. You must also know that it was I who filled that void in your heart by giving you another mother. Your mother-in-law taught you so many life lessons that you might have missed had I not given you that extra portion of grace. She taught you to cook; she was with you on all of those doctor visits when you were with child, and she loved you as if you were her own.*

KATHY. Oh my, yes, I don't know what I would have done without her. She was truly a blessing from you. I know for sure that she was the instrument you used to bring the joy back into my heart. You tell us in the book of James to "count it all joy when we meet trials of various kinds, for we know that the testing of our faith produces steadfastness." As I reflect on that today, I realize it was not the trials in my life that brought joy, but it was what you were doing through the trials. Is that right, God? You may have been testing my faith along with making it stronger.

GOD. *Such wisdom, Kathy! When you consider a trial joy, that is when you can rest in me and know that your future is secure. It is I who goes before you. I will be with you; I will not leave you or forsake you. Do not fear or be dismayed. I never left you for even a moment during that rainy season of your life. I was involved in every detail and was doing great things through the hurt.*

KATHY. God, I know my sweet mother-in-law is also there with you today. I wonder if both of my moms ever met and realized they had something in common. I will find out one day, but until then, I praise you and thank you for always looking out for me. I love you, Lord.

GOD. *I will leave you with something that I have told you many times before: "And your ears shall hear a word behind you, saying, this is the way, walk in it, when you turn to the right or when you turn to the left." Always be sensitive to my still small voice, and I will continue to lead and guide you in the rainy days ahead. That is a promise!*

KATHY. Thank you, God! I will be sure to look for the rainbow. Forever yours, Kathy.

Reflection of Today's Conversation

_____
_____
_____
_____
_____
_____

Scripture Application

- 2 Corinthians 1:3 says, "Blessed be the God and Father of our Lord Jesus Christ, the Father of mercies and God of all comfort." God wants to provide comfort to his children in any situation or circumstance they may face. All they need to do is ask.
- The twenty-third Psalm is very familiar to you if you grew up attending church. This Psalm gives us insight into the true character of God. Before David was a king, he was a shepherd who watched over his flock of sheep just as God is our shepherd and indeed watches over us. Today we will read each verse and discuss how God brings comfort to a hurting world.

Reflect on these individual verses. Go to https://healthychristian-home.com/psalm-23-meaning.

Mary gives us a beautiful personal interpretation of this beloved Psalm. See how she manages to bring each verse to life. Be sure to add your thoughts to it as well.

- The Lord is my Shepherd; I shall not want.
- He makes me lie down in green pastures. He leadeth me beside still waters. He restores my soul.
- He leads me in paths of righteousness for his name's sake.
- Even though I walk through the valley of the shadow of death, I will fear no evil, for you are with me; your rod and your staff, they comfort me.
- You prepare a table before me in the presence of my enemies.
- You anoint my head with oil; my cup overflows.
- Surely goodness and mercy shall follow me all the days of my life, and I shall dwell in the house of the Lord forever.

Wrap It Up

If you have not done so, I encourage you to commit this psalm to memory. It is one of the most popular psalms in the Bible, and it is a message of hope and healing when those rainy days are upon us. God ended the conversation with Kathy by reminding her to be attentive to that still small voice as he promises to continue to lead and guide her through the seasons of her life. Revelation 21:4 encourages us when it says,

> He will wipe away every tear from their eyes, and death shall be no more, neither shall there be mourning, nor crying, nor pain anymore, for the former things have passed away.

What an awesome promise from our Lord! Until that day comes, take all of your worries and rainy seasons to God, and be attentive to his voice, for he cares about the tiny details.

- Discussion
- Closing prayer

Father,

> Thank you for your love, grace, mercy, and goodness. Thank you that you are a God who comforts us no matter what we may be going through. We know you've seen our past, and we trust you with our future. We look forward to the day you wipe away every tear and we can dwell in your house forever.

Amen

The grace of the Lord Jesus Christ and the love of God and the fellowship of the Holy Spirit be with you all.

—2 Corinthians 13:14

Three in One

God my Creator
Jesus my Savior
Holy Spirit my Comforter
Three in one
A perfect union
Praise God who made the earth
Praise the Son who came through a miraculous birth
Who walked where men trod
Who died a horrible death
To save a wretch like me
Unworthy of His grace
But saved by it
Unworthy of His love
But thankful for it
Unworthy of His promises
But by grace through faith
God will love me into eternity
The three will meet me at the door
And forevermore
There will be Four

Kathy M. Crouch

CHAPTER 8

FINDING STRENGTH THROUGH DEATH

- Romans 8:28 ESV: "*And we know that for those who love God all things work together for good, for those who are called according to his purpose.*"
- Matthew 5:4 ESV: "*Blessed are those who mourn, for they shall be comforted.*"
- John 14:3 ESV: "*If I go and prepare a place for you, I will come again and take you to myself, that where I am you may be also.*"
- Philippians 1:21 ESV: "*For to me to live is Christ, and die is gain.*"

Let's Get Started

1. If you are a Christian, you know that the road you are traveling on is temporary. This is not your home. One day each one of us will pass from death to eternal life. We will be with our Lord forevermore. What are some of your feelings when dealing with death?

2. Have you lost anyone to death who was very close to you? What were some of the questions or concerns you had as you dealt with the loss?

3. Read *Romans 8:28*. How could these words bring you comfort when dealing with the death of someone you know? Do you think God uses trials and afflictions for good? If so, how? God knows everything about us, and he knows the end result. Do you think a person might actually grow closer to God through an illness?

4. Read *Matthew 5:4*. What does God say he will do for us when we are sad?

5. Read *John 14:3*. The promise in this verse makes it one of the most comforting verses in the Bible. Why?

6. Read *Philippians 1:21*. What does that verse say to you?

7. The conversation today covers actual events, and God showed Kathy how to have the kind of faith that is needed when losing someone near and dear to her. May you receive wisdom and insight from the reading.

A Conversation with God

KATHY. Dear God, death can often be a hard thing for me to wrap my mind around. As a Christian, I know that physical death is just the bridge to eternal life. I have just spent two years of my life watching my sister struggle with the loss of her husband. It has been hard, God. May we talk about this today?

GOD. *Sure, Kathy, death is something I happen to know a lot about. You can ask me anything.*

KATHY. My brother-in-law was one of the smartest men I knew. He was well read, always seemed to have the right answers; and when you opened the doors for him to become a pharmacist, so many people in this town followed him wherever he worked because he was not only a great pharmacist, he was a great listener and always gave well-received advice to those who went to see him. My sister was blessed to have him for so many years.

GOD. *Yes, George was very special to so many people. More importantly, he loved me with all of his heart. We had so many talks over the years, and he spent much of his time getting to know me better. He planted many seeds over the years, and yes, I made sure they grew. What seems to be bothering you at the moment concerning George?*

KATHY. Well, it's interesting to me that the one part of this very intelligent man to get sick was his mind. The disease that finally led to his death took away all that we once admired about him. At the end of his life here on earth, he struggled to feed himself, to walk, to speak, and finally, all communication ended. Lord, you know all of this that I am telling you. I just don't understand any of it. My sister had to endure these times, and even after you took him home, two years later, she is still trying to pick up the pieces and find the joy that she lost when he left.

GOD. *Okay, Kathy, this may take a little time for you to see things from my perspective, but before I give you any godly wisdom or insight on all of this, try to look back and remember the times you saw me during what I am quite sure you would describe as a rainy season.*

KATHY. Lord, I saw you many times. At the beginning of his illness, you opened up so many doors of opportunity for our families to travel together, creating wonderful memories, ones that my sister holds so dear today. I saw how you protected him when he often fell. He was such a tall man and he was never injured after the falls and you always sent angels to help pick him up. You gave my sister many months to get things in order and to grow stronger, knowing that it would be very difficult to care for him. The day I knew for sure you were there was when he couldn't carry on a conversation with me, but as I began reciting the Lord's prayer, he clearly and boldly joined in to help me finish. It was clear that those words meant something special to him. I could go on and on, but I think I get your point.

GOD. *All men are fallen beings with physical bodies prone to disease and illness. I need for you to know and understand that suffering and sickness are never easy to deal with. The one thing for sure is that these things should not cause you to question or lose faith in me. Since you love quotes so much, I need for you to remember the one by Max Lucado that I have heard you speak many times—the one about trusting me.*

KATHY. Yes, I love this quote. It says, "God is God. He knows what he is doing. When you can't trace his hand, trust his heart."

GOD. *Yes. "Never be afraid to leave an unknown future to a known God." Do you remember who said that, Kathy?*

KATHY. Yes, it was Corrie Ten Boom. She seems to have so much wisdom, Lord!

GOD. *That is the wisdom and insight I mentioned earlier. I can't think of anything better to sum it all up than those words. All men are born to die. Earthly bodies will eventually give way to death, but this is what I want you to know. Your future is in my hands. All things work together for good to those who love me and to those who are called according to my purpose. I have my purposes for allowing George to go through the trials and afflictions as he did, but George is alive and well. He is here ever so close to me. He has absolutely no regrets for the suffering he endured to get here. During his sickness, he grew closer to me, and he learned to trust me more. I am a sovereign God, and I knew the end result.*

KATHY. As I reflect back over the last few weeks of his life, I realize you were showing us your faithfulness. You made sure he was eventually in a good place surrounded by the people who loved him, and because of some of the decisions you guided my sister to make, he passed peacefully. The thing I am most thankful for is that he left here before the pandemic came. My sister would not have been allowed to be with him during his final days. Thank you for being so gracious to her. I still cherish the fact that the last person he heard before he took your hand was his pastor. He made it there just in time. Only you could have arranged that God. Again…no coincidence.

GOD. *Oh, I was there for sure. I whispered into your sweet brother-in-law's ear these words: "If I go and prepare a place for you, I will come again and receive you to myself; that where I am, you may be also." After that, you know the rest. I wiped away any tear from his eyes, and he is indeed resting in my arms. Take comfort in these words.*

KATHY. You always leave me speechless, Lord, but I am pretty sure that is your goal each time we meet. I have tried to comfort my sister the best way I know how, and it seems like she is beginning to find her joy again. Some days are better than others. Do you have words of comfort for her today?

GOD. *It is very simple. "Blessed are those who mourn, for they will be comforted." It will take time, but she will be okay. Your sister is strong. She talks to me each day, and she thanks me for giving her a sister who without she would be lost.*

KATHY. Wow! She's the best sister, and I thank you for her. George's life verse was "To live is Christ, and to die is gain." He ran the race, and he finished well, didn't he, God?

GOD. *He did indeed!*

KATHY. Thank you, and praise you, Lord. I know we will see George again, and we look forward to a great reunion. Thanks for your faithfulness to us, and may we learn through times like these to have the kind of faith that also came from the words of Corrie Ten Boom: "Faith sees the invisible, believes the unbelievable, and receives the impossible." Oh, to have faith like that! I bet George did. Love, Kathy.

Reflection of Today's Conversation

_____

_____

_____

_____

_____

_____

Scripture Application

- John 3:16 says, "For God so loved the world that he gave his only begotten son, that whosoever believes in him should not perish but have eternal life." This is a verse that is well known among believers and gives us hope of a life after this one. Have we taken the time to contemplate the depth of truth this verse holds? God, who is love, demonstrated his love through his only begotten Son, Jesus Christ. Through him, he offered salvation to all mankind. What a gift!

- There are many verses in the Bible that speak to us concerning what happens once we pass from death to eternal life. We will look at some of those today.
- Read these verses to discover these truths, and discuss your thoughts after reading them.
  o *John 11:25, 26*
  o *1 Corinthians 15: 42–44*
  o *2 Corinthians 4:16–18; 5:1–8*
  o *Romans 14:8*
- The book of Revelation offers us so much hope as we stare into the face of death: *Revelation 1:17, 18; Revelation 14:13; Revelation 21:4.*
- In closing, read *1 Thessalonians 4:13–18.* How should we encourage each other with these words?

Wrap It Up

Max Lucado said it best when he said:

> I think the command which puts an end to the pains of earth and initiates the joys of heaven will be two words. No more! The King of Kings will raise his pierced hand and proclaim no more! No more loneliness, no more tears, no more death, no more pain.

I must agree with him. He went on to say:

> You're on a land mine, my friend, and it's only a matter of time. The next time you are tossed into a river as you ride the rapids of life, remember the words of assurance. Those who

endure will be saved. The gospel will be preached. The end will come. You can count on it.

When our brief life is over on this earth, let us find comfort in the fact that God has indeed prepared a place for those who love him, and we will be with him forever.

- Discussion
- Closing prayer

Father,

> You willingly gave yourself up to death so that all might be saved and pass from death to life. We thank you for that. When you call one of our loved ones home to be with you, it leaves us with a void that only you can fill until we see them again. We ask and pray that you will help us to focus on the sweet memories instead of focusing on the loss. Thank you for the promises of heaven once we put our trust in you.

Amen

For his anger is but for a moment, and his favor is for a lifetime. Weeping may tarry for the night, but joy comes in the morning.

—Psalm 30:5

Joy Comes in the Morning

The steadfast love of the Lord never ends.
New mercies each morning, God faithfully sends.
When troubles and sadness appear in the night,
New mercies are coming through miraculous light.
The light that doth shine at the dawn of each day,

Brings the Joy that will take all of our burdens away.
Christ is that light where the joy enters in,
And captures our hearts from without and within.
So as night creeps in with burdens to bear,
The morning star will soon be there.
Joy comes in the morning; it will not delay.
Cast all of your cares upon Jesus today.

Kathy M. Crouch

CHAPTER 9

ANGELS

- Psalm 91:11 ESV: "*For he will command his angels concerning you to guard you in all your ways.*"
- Matthew 18:10 ESV: "*See that you do not despise one of these little ones. For I tell you that in heaven their angels always see the face of my Father who is in heaven.*"
- Proverbs 16:9 ESV: "*In their hearts, humans plan their course, but it is God that establishes their steps.*"

Let's Get Started

1. What are your thoughts concerning angels?
2. Has there ever been a time in your life when you were sure an angel was watching over you?
3. List some instances in the Bible where angels were mentioned.
4. The Bible tells us that angels were witnesses to the creation of the world. They were created to do God's will, to be his instruments to carry out his work. This means that they were created even before the world came into existence. Do you know what the word *angel* actually means? It means "messenger or agent." How does God use angels as his messengers? Give examples of when God used angels as messengers in the Bible.

5. Read *Psalm 91:11*. What does this verse reveal about God's purpose for the angels in our lives?

6. Read *Matthew 18:10*. Jesus affirms the existence of angels in this verse. What does it tell you about the possibility of guardian angels interceding on our behalf?

7. Have you ever reflected on some of the foolish, maybe even dangerous choices you've made in the past and now feel like there must have been an angel watching over you during those times?

8. Read *Proverbs 16:9*. What role would angels play when we consider this verse?

A Conversation with God

KATHY. Dear God, I was reading Psalm 91, and verse 11 really spoke to me. "For he will command his angels concerning you to guard you in all your ways." Then I read in Matthew's gospel, "See that you do not despise one of these little ones. For I tell you that in heaven their angels always see the face of my Father who is in heaven." I have heard about angels since I was a little girl. They have always fascinated me. Could we talk about that today?

GOD. *Well, angels are very real, Kathy. They are fascinating spiritual beings. They praise and worship me while also protecting and directing my children. They were created at the same time the earth was formed, even before human life was created. Though you might not see them, just know they are there.*

KATHY. Lord, was there an angel watching over me that day I was waiting for my mom to pick me up from my junior high school? You know, when that man drove up and said that my mom had sent him to get me?

GOD. *Yes, I was not about to let you get in that car.*

KATHY. That man sounded so nice and looked very kind, but something or someone told me not to go with him. I was extremely shy as a child, so I very politely told him that my mother would be there soon, and he drove off. I was too young to give that a lot of thought, but as I have grown up, gotten married, and had children of my own, it has weighed heavily on my heart. Why did you do it, God? Why me? There are so many children that were not so fortunate.

GOD. *I told you in an earlier conversation that my ways are not your ways and sometimes my purposes are often hard to comprehend. Just know that I have a special measure of grace reserved for those whom I call home at an early age. I chose to protect you that day.*

KATHY. I can think back over my life, and there were so many times where I acted foolishly and probably shouldn't be alive today. I don't need to go into much detail as you already know exactly what I mean. There is no doubt you have a purpose for my life.

GOD. *Yes, remember, in their hearts, humans plan their course, but it is I that establishes their steps. If you recall, you had chosen a different path for yourself, and I had to intervene. I am sure we will talk about this path in another conversation.*

KATHY. Yes, we definitely will, but I have a few more questions about angels. My pastor told his congregation about a time he was swimming in the ocean and an undercurrent began to carry him out and under. He believes to this day that a stranger appeared and helped him break free. He described how the face, the glow, and the peace that this stranger possessed were things he could not explain. He often reflects back on that day. This stranger was never seen again. Could this have been one of your angels?

GOD. *Most definitely! He needed a warrior that day, so I sent the stranger. When you get to heaven, you will probably be amazed to discover just how often my angels protected you and those around you. Whether you realize it or not, angels are watching over you at this very moment.*

KATHY. Lord, you bring so much comfort to my life as you help me to understand spiritual things more clearly. You had your hands full during the childhood days of my husband and his brother. There is no doubt that angels were looking over them and their mother as well. The stories they tell all lead to the fact that angels are real and you most definitely have a plan and purpose for their lives.

GOD. *Yes, those two have kept me pretty busy. I often heard the prayers of their mother. She was indeed a prayer warrior, and she knew about the angels.*

KATHY. I would like to end our conversation today with one of my favorite quotes. Dr. David Jeremiah said, "What a loving God we serve. He prepared a heavenly dwelling for us, but his angels also accompany us as we transition from this world to the next." Wow! Not only are they watching over us here but they will also come get us when our life is over here.

GOD. *Yes, and they will tenderly accompany you into my presence.*

KATHY. Thank you for the angels, God; but most of all, thank you for your Son, Jesus. It is by believing in him that makes all of this possible. I will talk to you again tomorrow. This might be a good time to discuss the path I took to get here. Love always, Kathy.

Reflection of Today's Conversation

_____

_____

_____

_____

_____

_____

Scripture Application

- Billy Graham had many things to say concerning angels. He said, "When my time to die comes, an angel will be there to comfort me." He also said, "Believers, look up— take courage. The angels are nearer than you think." What are your thoughts as you read these quotes?
- Genesis 2:1 says, "Thus the heavens and the earth were completed in all their vast array." Angels are spiritual beings created by God, and they dwell in heaven with him and serve him. How does this fact comfort you?

- When Jesus was in the garden of Gethsemane, he received comfort and strength from an angel. He knew he was going to die a horrific death for all humanity. Read *Luke 22:43–44.* Christ retreated to this garden in a time of agony before his arrest and crucifixion. How can this account of an angel comfort us and give us hope?
- Read these scriptures, and discover more about the angels.
  - *John 20:11–13; Matthew 28:2–7*
  - *Revelation 5:11, 12; Hebrews 13:2*
  - *Luke 1:11–13; Matthew 24:31, 36*
  - *Matthew 16:27; Matthew 25:31–36*

Wrap It Up

As we can see from the scriptures, angels are very real. They were present at the tomb when Christ rose from the dead, and they will accompany him in his return. They watch over us; and if we know Christ Jesus as our Lord and Savior, he will send an angel to accompany us to heaven on our final day. Hebrews 13:2 reminds us to "show hospitality to strangers, for thereby some have entertained angels unawares."

- Discussion
- Closing prayer

Father,

Thank you for this conversation concerning angels. Thank you that they watch over us each day. May they continue to surround us and protect us as you guide us in the way we should go. Keep us ever mindful to show kindness and hospitality to those less fortunate than ourselves, realizing that they could very well be angels.

Amen

Angels

Before the world was created
There were angels
Applauding, and praising the one
True God
Who made it all
Dwelling in the heavens
Messengers
Agents
Created to do God's will
To watch over us
To comfort us
To at times, keep us safe
Nearer than we think
Angelic beings
Who were present at the tomb
Who will accompany him in his return
Should this day be our last
It will be an angel
To come take us by the hand
And lead us to the promised land
To be with our Savior
Forever
Thank you, God
For the angels

Kathy M. Crouch

Chapter 10

LIFE'S PATH

- Proverbs 3:5, 6 ESV: "*Trust in the Lord with all your heart; and do not lean on your own understanding, in all your ways acknowledge him and he will make straight your paths.*"
- Proverbs 6:23 ESV: "*For the commandment is like a lamp and the teaching; a light; and the reproofs of discipline are the way of life.*"
- 2 Corinthians 5:17 ESV: "*If anyone believes in me, he is a new creation. The old has passed away; behold, the new has come.*"
- Proverbs 16:9 ESV: "*The heart of man plans his way, but the Lord establishes their steps.*"
- Psalm 37:4 ESV: "*Delight yourself in the Lord, and he will give you the desires of your heart.*"

Let's Get Started

1. In the journey of life, there will be many paths to take. Have you ever thought about your life as being on a path going somewhere? If so, please explain.
2. Think about the path you have taken. Which word or words would best describe your path thus far (smooth,

curvy, bumpy, straight, hard, long, steep)? What have been some of the factors that led you down that particular path?

3. Billy Graham said, "My home is in heaven. I'm just traveling through this world." Have you ever considered your path of life from that perspective—a path being traveled in a land you are just visiting?

4. Read *Proverbs 3:5, 6*. How powerful are these words in helping us to understand that God knows what is best for us on this journey we are on? What could be the results of leaning unto our own understanding as we travel down life's path?

5. Read *Proverbs 6:23*. Unpack this verse as it relates to life's path (commandment, lamp, light, discipline). How could this verse help keep us on the right path?

6. Read *2 Corinthians 5:17*. How does this verse fit into today's lesson? How can that one decision direct our steps?

7. Read *Proverbs 16:9*. What are your thoughts here? Are you a planner? Because we cannot see the future, how does this verse bring comfort to us as we continue down our path of life?

8. Read *Psalm 37:4*. What will be the advantages of keeping our eyes focused on the Lord and desiring his will for our life as we move forward in the days to come?

A Conversation with God

KATHY. Dear God, I mentioned to you yesterday that I might like to talk to you about the path I took in life to bring me to this very place. As I study your Word, the word *path* is mentioned in many places. That leads me to believe that it is important. The psalmist talked about a path numerous times, but one of my favorite verses comes from Proverbs, which is the very reason I would like to find out more about it. It says, "Trust in the Lord with all your heart, and do not lean on your own understanding. In all your ways acknowledge him, and he will make straight your paths."

GOD. *Yes, there are many references to a path in my Word, and it should not be taken lightly. It is very important that I lead and direct because choosing the right path is of the utmost importance. Many times, leaning unto your own understanding can lead one in the wrong direction.*

KATHY. In the book of Proverbs, Solomon wrote "For the commandment is like a lamp and the teaching a light, and the reproofs of discipline are the way of life." Max Lucado said, "Reading Proverbs turns on the lamps in the dark corners of life." I never really thought about Scripture that way, but it speaks volumes to me.

GOD. *When you read the Psalms, they will tell you how to get along with me. Proverbs tells you how to get along with other people. Both are very important. From the day you were born, there was a path set before you. I, however, gave you the choice to follow me or to go your own way. Reading Scripture helps guide you along the way.*

KATHY. Okay, I would like to talk a little about my path if that's okay with you. I am sure it was very curvy! I was very fortunate to find you at an early age, and as I reflect back over the years after the decision to follow you, I must confess that I don't think I prayed enough or asked for direction the way I understand it now.

GOD. *Kathy, you were young, and I knew that. I knew you were weak, but the day you asked me into your heart, I filled you with the Holy Spirit who helped to lead you and make you into the person you are today. You put your trust in me, and if anyone believes in me and asks me into their heart, he is a new creation. The old has passed away; behold, the new has come.*

KATHY. I am so thankful for my decision to follow you, Lord. When did you decide I would become a teacher? I was really into the arts and wanted to do something entirely different.

GOD. *I introduced you to your husband, and then his sister had much to do about that.*

KATHY. Oh yes, for sure. I admired her passion for teaching young children, and that is when I changed course. The path changed, but I still don't remember praying or talking it over with you. I feel like I let you down and you took care of me anyway.

GOD. *I told you in one of our previous conversations that the heart of man plans his way, but I establish their steps. I knew that the elementary school you attended as a child needed a good first-grade teacher. Only I could have arranged for you to teach first grade in the very room you sat in as a first grader. I indeed directed your path.*

KATHY. That is so awesome, God. I did think that was very odd. That is one of those things that was not a coincidence. You gave me thirty wonderful years there and the opportunity to touch hundreds of young precious lives. I have often joked that my school should become a retirement home so I can finish out my years there! I am so glad I met my sister-in-law. It would not have happened had you not allowed me to meet Jeff. Can you tell me more about how you led us both down that particular path?

GOD. *Yes, Jeff prayed to find you. It was extremely important to him that he find and marry a Christian girl, and so I led him down the path that brought him to you and then down the path to your heart.*

KATHY. This seemed to be a pattern with me, God. I am so humbled right now. I am pretty sure I failed you there as well.

GOD. *Kathy, I am far more interested in what comes from inside. Though your words may have been few during that time, I could hear what was on your heart and mind. Your desires were the same as his, and that is what led you both down the same path. Remember, you were headed down a different path, and it was I that turned you around.*

KATHY. Thank you, God. I can't imagine any other path but the one I am on at this very moment. You have blessed me beyond measure over these many years, and I am so truly grateful. Thank you for explaining my journey and for showing me how important prayer is in every decision we make.

GOD. *Remember, as long as you continue to delight yourself in me, I will give you the desires of your heart.*

KATHY. Thank you for that, Lord. That means everything to me. You have given me so much to think about. Forever yours, Kathy.

Reflection of Today's Conversation

_____

_____

_____

_____

_____

_____

Scripture Application

- Making plans for the future is a wise thing to do. God gave us free will to choose the path we will take while on our journey here on earth. If we are a child of God, he will often use the Holy Spirit to rearrange our plans; but in doing so, it will be for our own good because he knows everything about us, and his ways are perfect. He will always bring us to a place of fulfillment that we may not have thought possible.

- Read _James 4:13–17_. These verses speak to us about planning our lives or establishing our steps. Choosing our path is crucial, and it will never be everything God desires it to be if we try to accomplish it without him. James is telling us that we have no idea what tomorrow will bring, and it would be best to ask what God's will would be for us. Our future lies not in our hands but in the hands of our Lord. What are your thoughts when reading these verses from James?

- Read _Matthew 6:25–34_. How do these verses reassure us that God will take care of us and lead us when choosing our path?

- Read _Psalm 16:11_. What truths are found in this verse if we remain in God's presence and keep walking with God on his path? How can you be sure you are on the right path today?

Wrap It Up

Living a self-sufficient life can lead us down the wrong path. We are as a vapor—here today and gone tomorrow. God sees our tomorrows and knows what is best for us. As we begin to ask for God's will to be done in our lives, we must be planning our eternal future as well. Matthew 6:19, 20 tells us to store up our treasures in heaven, not on earth. What does that mean?

There is going to be a gate that Christians will go through one day, and the road (path) will be very narrow or very wide. In closing, we will read *Matthew 7:13, 14.*

- Discussion
- Closing prayer

Father,

Thank you that we have the freedom to choose our path, but thank you most of all for revealing to us through your Word the importance of having you establish our steps. We pray for the wisdom to make the right choices as we seek your will in all that we do. May the Holy Spirit rule and overrule in every decision we make in the days ahead.

Amen

Lean not unto your own understanding, but in all thy ways acknowledge him and he will direct your path.

—Proverbs 3:5, 6

He Leadeth Me

Though my path is long with twists and turns,
My Savior leadeth me.
He holds my hand, he guides each step,
And whispers
Follow me.
Okay, I say, not knowing where,
My Savior leadeth me.
He looks ahead, he clears the path,
And whispers
Follow me.
He feels my steps, he knows they're weak,
He whispers
Follow me.
I try so hard, I'm still not sure,
My Savior lifteth me.
He gently turns, his eyes meet mine,
He whispers
I'll carry thee.

Kathy M. Crouch

CHAPTER 11

PRAYER

- Ephesians 2:8 ESV: "*For by grace you have been saved through faith and this is not of your own doing, it is a gift from God.*"
- Luke 22:42 ESV: "*Father, if you are willing, remove this cup from me. Nevertheless, not my will, but yours be done.*"
- Jeremiah 29:11 ESV: "*For I know the plans I have for you, plans for welfare and not for evil, to give you a future and a hope.*"

Let's Get Started

1. When you were a child, did you say a particular prayer before you went to sleep? Would you like to share it today?
2. What is prayer? On a scale from 1–10, 1 being the lowest, how important do you think prayer is to the Christian life?
3. When you pray, do you pray according to God's will? What would that mean?
4. Read *Ephesians 2:8*. How would genuine faith fit into this scripture?
5. Read *Luke 22:42*. Do you ever consider the fact that even Jesus prayed? What was his ultimate goal in this particular prayer? Does that help clarify what it means to pray according to God's will?

6. Read *Jeremiah 29:11*. What does this tell us about God's plans for our life? Why is prayer so important if God already knows his plans for us?

7. What are some things you don't understand about prayer that you hope this conversation clears up for you?

A Conversation with God

KATHY. Dear God, when I was a little girl, I would recite this prayer each night before I drifted off to sleep. "Father, we thank thee for the night and for the pleasant morning light, for rest and food and love and care and all that makes the world so fair. Amen." When I got a little older, I learned the one that said, "Now I lay me down to sleep; I pray the Lord my soul to keep. If I should die before I wake, I pray the Lord my soul to take. Amen."

GOD. *Yes, I remember those days as well. You would add at the end bless Mama and Daddy and your Uncle Norman, who lived with you at the time. Children's prayers are very precious to me. I use them to reveal myself to them.*

KATHY. Those two prayers are very different. The first one seems to be a prayer of praise for the things you have provided, and the second one focuses on the soul and the assurance of heaven should one die before they wake. These prayers hold a special place in my heart as a reminder that even as a child, I was taught to talk to you at the end of each day, and it always gave me peace and helped me sleep better. It is only now that I even focused on how different these two prayers really are. It might have been good to have had them both at the same time!

GOD. *Kathy, sometimes you make me laugh. Remember, it is the heart where I reside, and the most important thing is the message. You were seeking me with heartfelt prayers to give you a good night's rest and acknowledge that I exist. That is what mattered to me the most. I know that you also taught your own children to learn these prayers. That is how a prayer life begins and takes root as one grows older.*

KATHY. Could we talk a little bit about prayer today?

GOD. *Of course. Prayer is important, and I speak about it throughout the Bible.*

KATHY. I know that prayer is having a conversation with you. I know you enjoy hearing from your children, and I know how much comfort it brings to me when I pray. I have learned through our conversations that it is not only important to talk to you, but listening to you is of the utmost importance. I am really trying to work on that.

GOD. *Kathy, by grace you have been saved through faith, and this is not of your own doing; it is a gift from me. This is where genuine prayer comes from. It is that faith you have in my Son, Jesus. It is used to develop a relationship with me. How much would you know about your husband or best friend if you never communicated with them? The same goes for me. We have to talk to get to know each other.*

KATHY. I know there are many things that can be discussed when it comes to one's prayer life, but this quote caught my attention today. L. B. Cowman said, "Nothing lies beyond the reach of prayer except those things outside the will of God." I had to read that several times before it could sink in. Please talk to me about the outside of your will part.

GOD. *Anything you pray must be according to my divine will. That is very hard for many people to grasp and hold on to.*

KATHY. How would I best explain that to someone who might not understand?

GOD. *Praying my will is being honest with me about what you are asking for but also surrendering your life and outcome of your prayer to me. You must be willing to align your life with my will more than your desire. I see your future, and I will always know what is best for you.*

KATHY. It says in the twenty-second chapter of Luke that Jesus withdrew from his disciples to pray. That is such an awesome image when I really think about it. He knew he would suffer a horrible death for the sake of mankind. He prayed what any one of us might have prayed when facing death, but he surrendered his will to your will. That's what you mean, isn't it, Lord? Then he said, "Father, if you are willing, remove this cup from me; nevertheless, not my will but yours be done."

GOD. *Yes, my son gave you the perfect example of what that means. Just as I had a plan for my son, I have a sovereign purpose and plan for each human being. I have only revealed as much of my will to you as you need to know at this moment. The duration of your life is unknown to you and in my hands. For I know the plans I have for you, plans for welfare and not for evil, to give you a future and a hope. Just remember to pray often, ask for my wisdom, believe, trust, and have faith. My will for your life will be perfect. The more you get to know me through reading my Word and prayer time, the easier it will be to trust in my promises and will for your life.*

KATHY. Right now, I must confess I haven't prayed nearly enough for your will to be done in my life. I am so sorry, God.

GOD. *That is okay, and I forgive you. That is the hard part for many of my children. The important thing is that you know how to move forward.*

KATHY. Thank you for our talk today. I wrote you a little poem. May your will be done in my life, o God, as I learn to trust you more. May my prayers reveal my love for you as never seen before. Love, Kathy.

Reflection of Today's Conversation

_____

_____

_____

_____

_____

_____

Scripture Application

- Paul David Tripp stated, "Prayer is never about asking God to submit his awesome power to your will and your plan;

prayer is an act of personal submission to the always-right will of God." What does that say to you today?

- Read *Matthew 6:9–13*. This scripture is very familiar to Christians all around the world. Jesus taught this as the way to pray. Praying God's will means we are making a promise to God that we will obey his wishes or commands on earth. His wishes will be completed on earth just as they are in heaven. What makes it so hard for us to relinquish our will to the will of God?

[handwritten note in margin: Lord's Prayer]

- The Bible has much to say to us about prayer. Corrie Ten Boom said, "Is prayer your steering wheel or your spare tire?" Let that sink in for a moment. What are your thoughts here? She also said, "What wings are to a bird and sails to a ship, so are prayers to the soul." Thoughts?
- Read these verses about prayer, and reflect on them.
  o *Philippians 4:13*
  o *1 Thessalonians 5:16–18*
  o *Jeremiah 33:3, 29:12*
  o *Matthew 6:5–8, 7:7*
  o *1 John 5:14*
  o *1 Timothy 2:5*
- Charles Spurgeon said this: "We must pray to pray and continue in prayer so our prayers may continue." That can be captured in the verse from 1 Thessalonians 5:17. Pray without ceasing. Read this quote several times, and see if it resonates in your heart and brings new meaning to your thoughts on prayer.
- I will close with one of my favorite quotes by L. B. Cowman: "Pray until what you pray for has been accomplished or until you have complete assurance in your heart that it will be. Only when one of these two conditions has been met is it safe to stop persisting in prayer."

Wrap It Up

- Discussion

- Closing prayer

Father,

Thank you for teaching us that prayer is essential to the Christian life. As we learn to talk to you more, help us to listen as well. May we learn to step outside of our will and into yours. Cover us with your grace and mercy as we grow closer to you in the days ahead.

Amen

Then you will call on me and come and pray
to me, and I will listen to you.

—Jeremiah 29:12

A Childhood Prayer

Now I lay me down to sleep,
I pray the Lord my soul to keep.
These are the words I prayed as a child,
As I was tucked in at night to go to sleep.
If I should die before I wake,
I pray the Lord my soul to take.
These are the words that completed my prayer,
I did not know what was really at stake.
At the end of each day do I bow my head,
Do I consider it might be my last?
Do I remember the blessings he gave me that day;
Or do I drift off to sleep really fast?
Does my childhood prayer still ring true today;
Though the words may not be quite the same?
Before I close my eyes at night,
Do I tenderly call him by name?

Do I pray and ask God to keep my soul,
Tucked away in the shelter of his wings?
If I should die before I wake,
Would I be with the King of Kings?
Now I lay me down to sleep,
I pray the Lord my soul to keep.
If I should die before I wake,
I pray the Lord my soul to take.
A simple prayer I will pray again,
For today it means much more to me.
Should I die before the new day dawns,
It's my Savior I long to see.

Kathy M. Crouch

CHAPTER 12

ENCOURAGEMENT

- 2 Corinthians 12:9 ESV: *"My grace is sufficient for you. My strength is made perfect through weakness."*
- Matthew 5:4 ESV: *"Blessed are those who morn, for they shall be comforted."*
- Psalm 34:18 ESV: *"The Lord is near to the brokenhearted and saves the crushed in spirit."*
- Proverbs 8:17 ESV: *"I love those who love me and those who seek me diligently will find me."*

Let's Get Started

1. Have there been people in your past who have encouraged you when you were going through tough times?
2. Can you think of an incident where out of nowhere you received encouragement through a letter, text, phone call, etc.?
3. Have you ever thought that maybe God puts people in our path at a particular time for a particular purpose? During a difficult time in your life, have you been somewhere and run into someone special whom you haven't seen in a very long time? Do you think God may have had a reason for arranging the meeting that day?

4. Read *2 Corinthians 12:9*. What does this verse say to you? God was reminding Paul that the strength behind his ministry was only made possible through his grace. God's grace is sufficient when we are weak. When we are weak in whatever we try to accomplish for God's kingdom here on earth, God's strength is even more evident. Can you think of a time when you knew that God was the strength behind a certain task you were given?

5. Read *Matthew 5:4*. What do you think about when you hear the word *mourn*? What or whom have you mourned over? How does God comfort us during these difficult times?

6. Read *Psalm 34:18*. How does it feel knowing that God is near to us when our hearts are broken?

7. Read *Proverbs 8:17*. What are your thoughts concerning this verse?

A Conversation with God

KATHY. Dear God, I've been wondering a lot lately about how you use other people to encourage us when we are going through tough times.

GOD. *Yes, Kathy, what is it that has you pondering this fact?*

KATHY. Well, there have been times when out of nowhere, someone would write, send a text, or call at the exact time I needed to be encouraged. Sometimes I would run into someone in a store who I hadn't seen in a long time and we would have really good conversations and I always left feeling better than before we talked.

GOD. *Sometimes I put people in your path for a purpose. It might be for them to comfort you, or I may need for you to be the comforter. It is important to be sensitive to my voice during these times.*

KATHY. Thank you for using Kate to bring comfort to me last month.

GOD. *Yes, you have a very special granddaughter in that one.*

KATHY. I was having a hard time trying to cope with the fact that if you decide not to return and decide to leave us here a little longer, my grandchildren will grow up in a country much different than the one I remember. I know how much you love little children, and so I know you understand how I feel.

GOD. *Yes, I do love the little children, and I love you as well. I knew you needed to hear from me, so as I stated earlier, I had a purpose for Kate. She is wise beyond her years. I knew she was the one who would be sensitive to my still small voice.*

KATHY. Lord, you also knew that when I received my journal two years ago, it would be the tool to bring it all together, didn't you?

GOD. *Yes, I certainly did.*

KATHY. I remember Kate asking about the journal over the Christmas holidays and I told her that I used it to record quotes, and of course, that's when I had to explain what a quote was. After all, she is only six.

GOD. *Kathy, always remember that my grace is sufficient for you and my strength is made perfect through weakness. Although Kate is only six years old, I chose her to show you and others that I can use anyone of any age to accomplish my great eternal purpose. Read Kate's journal to me. I would like to hear it again.*

KATHY. Okay, Lord. It says, "Follow the Lord God with all your heart and all your mind no matter what forever and ever. Dedicated to my grandma. I love you with all my heart! Pray to the Lord!"

GOD. *Did you notice where she signed her name?*

KATHY. Yes! That's when the tears came! As you know, this journal has scripture at the bottom of each page; and on this particular page, it said, "The Lord is near to the brokenhearted, Kathy, and saves the crushed in spirit." She signed her name right there! Wow, God! I was so brokenhearted on the day I picked up this journal. It was the end of January, and I hadn't looked in it since Christmas.

GOD. *That was my perfect plan. I knew when you would need it. Blessed are those who mourn, for they shall be comforted. I am the great comforter. So, which part spoke to you the most?*

KATHY. It was when she said, "No matter what." Then she added, "For ever and ever." I clearly see that you were in and through this whole thing, God. I have learned from a child that I must lean on you regardless of what this world may be going through and that you will take care of my precious grandchildren—no matter what!

GOD. *Remember, Kathy, I love those who love me, and those who seek me diligently will find me. It may be that you find me in the secret places of your heart, places you never knew were there. It may be through small acts of kindness or through those you least expect. If you let me, I will love you into eternity—no matter what! Forever and ever!*

KATHY. I am a little overwhelmed after this conversation, Lord. There is much to take in and much to consider. Thank you that I have your ear and that you not only listen, but you care. Most of all, thank you for leaving me with a blessed assurance that you are who you say you are and that I matter. I love you, Lord! Kathy.

Reflection of Today's Conversation

_____

_____

_____

_____

_____

_____

Scripture Application

- The definition of *encouragement* is "the action of giving someone support, confidence, or hope." We all need support and encouragement. Many people in the Bible felt like giving up from time to time, but God encouraged them.
  o When Moses was overwhelmed, God appointed his brother Aaron to help him.
  o When Job had lost everything, God ultimately blessed him in his later years.

- o After Hannah poured out her heart to God, he opened up her womb, and she gave birth to a son.
- o When Elijah ran for his life, God met him and assured him he was not alone.
- Read *Romans 15:4*. Encouragement gives us hope.
- Read *John 13:34, 35*. God's commandment encourages us to love.
- Read *John 10:10*. God encourages us with abundant life if we choose to follow him.
- Read *1 Thessalonians 5:9–11*. How do these verses encourage us to continue encouraging others?
- There was a man in the Bible whose nickname was "Son of Encouragement." Read *Acts 11:22–24*. Everything he did was done to help people follow Jesus. Who was this man?
- Read *Acts 9:26–31* to see Barnabas's encouragement in action. What was it in verse 31 that was the source of encouragement to the believers? What was the result? Read *Acts 15:36–39* to see how he was an encourager to Mark by standing up for him.

Wrap it Up

Encouragement is something we all need. Second Corinthians 1:3–5 says:

> Blessed be the God and Father of our Lord Jesus Christ, the Father of mercies and God of all comfort, who comforts us in all our affliction so that we may be able to comfort those who are in any affliction, with the comfort with which we ourselves are comforted by God. For as we share abundantly in Christ's sufferings, so through Christ we share abundantly in comfort too.

The word *encouragement* is replaced with *comfort*. Because God comforts us, we can comfort others. Look for ways and opportunities to encourage or comfort someone in the days ahead. Just as God used a six-year-old child to comfort Kathy on one of her darkest days, he can use you to shine a light into someone else's life if only you will let him.

- Discussion
- Closing prayer

Father,

We pray today that you will instill in us the importance of comforting and encouraging those around us who may be going through difficult times. May the indwelling of your Spirit help us to be sensitive to the needs of others. Thank you for loving us and for being a God of encouragement.

Amen

The Lord is near to the brokenhearted and saves the crushed in spirit.

—Psalm 34:18

A Comforting Heart

At the end of each day
Can I honestly say,
I encouraged someone
And brought comfort their way?
Did I smile, did I listen
Did I reach out and touch?
Do I have what it takes
To love others that much?
At the end of each day
Did I genuinely care,

For the people I met
Who had burdens to bear?
In the depths of my heart
Does my Jesus live there?
Does he rule does he reign
Is he in there somewhere?
O God please create
A clean heart inside me.
Mold and reshape it
As you desire it to be.
As I yield to your spirit
And begin a new day,
May I encourage someone
And bring comfort their way.

Kathy M. Crouch

CHAPTER 13

SEED PLANTERS

- Matthew 13: 4–8 ESV: "*When the seeds were planted, some seeds fell along the path, and the birds came and devoured them. Other seeds fell on rocky ground, where they did not have much soil, and immediately they sprang up, since they had no depth in the soil. But when the sun rose, they were scorched, and since they had no root, they withered away. Other seeds fell among thorns, and the thorns grew up and choked them. Other seeds fell on good soil and produced grain, some a hundred-fold, some sixty, some thirty.*"
- 1 Corinthians 3:7 ESV: "*So neither he who plants nor he who waters is anything, but only God who gives growth.*"

Let's Get Started

1. What comes to your mind when you hear the words *seed planter*? Have you ever planted seeds? When seeds are planted, what is needed to make them grow?
2. Do you remember a parable in the Bible where Jesus spoke about planting seeds? Read *Matthew 13:4–8*. Discuss the different types of soil the seeds were planted in.
3. What kind of garden would we have if we planted our seeds in these types of soil?

4. What happened when the seeds were planted in good soil? Why do you think Jesus was teaching this lesson to the crowd gathered around him? What do you think the seeds represent in this parable? (We will read the rest of the parable during the Scripture application to discover the importance of each type of soil and what they represent.)

5. Have you ever considered yourself to be a planter of something other than an actual seed? If so, what would that be?

6. Have you ever given or received anything that contained the Word of God—a Bible, devotional, card, email, etc.? How could the person giving one or more of these items be considered a seed planter?

7. Read *1 Corinthians 3:7*. How does this scripture separate God from the one who plants the seeds?

A Conversation with God

KATHY. Dear God, I love devotionals and quotes. Thank you for inspiring men and women to write words of encouragement, and thank you for all of the devotionals that I have been given over the years and for giving me opportunities to give them away as well.

GOD. *Yes, Kathy, you might say I created the seed planter.*

KATHY. What is a seed planter?

GOD. *When anything is given away that contains my Word, a seed has been planted that has the potential to change lives. But you must always remember, neither he who plants nor he who waters are anything but only I who causes growth.*

KATHY. I am a little confused, God. Could you explain that a little more?

GOD. *Do you remember the parable of the Sower? A farmer sowed his seed indiscriminately. Devotionals are sometimes given to others indiscriminately. There may have been a reason and purpose behind your thinking when you gave these books away, but sometimes they are bought in a store or handed down after being read or maybe just discarded.*

KATHY. Yes, I bought several one year and then decided whom to give them to. But there have been times when I bought them and had a particular person in mind. Is that what you mean?

GOD. *Let me continue with the parable. When the seeds were planted, some seeds fell along the path, and the birds came and devoured them. Other seeds fell on rocky ground where they did not have much soil, and immediately they sprang up since they had no depth in the soil. But when the sun rose, they were scorched; and since they had no root, they withered away. Other seeds fell among thorns, and the thorns grew up and choked them. Other seeds fell on good soil and produced grain, some a hundredfold, some sixty, some thirty.*

KATHY. So, are you saying that all of the devotionals I have given away have not been sown on good soil?

GOD. *What I am saying is that I used you to plant as many seeds as possible, but it is I who will see that it grows. It will happen in my time and in my way. There are choices to be made, and not all soil is fertile.*

KATHY. Sometimes I go looking in a closet or drawer or on a bookshelf and see a book I have never noticed before, and I take it, flip through the pages, and decide it would be a good read. I have been blessed so many times when that happened. It never occurred to me that it was a seed planted for me to find.

GOD. *Remember in our last conversation, I used Kate to plant the seed in your journal, and I knew the exact minute you would need it. That is when you picked it up. The soil was good. Listen, you may never know on this side of heaven who actually reads one of your gifts or the impact that it had on their life. You may never know the type of soil it was planted in. The most important thing for you to know is that you planted the seed. I will always do the rest.*

KATHY. May I share one of my quotes with you that comes to mind as you so beautifully taught me what it means to put my trust in you and have faith that the seeds I may plant will bear fruit according to your will?

GOD. *Sure, I would love to hear it.*

KATHY. It is a very short quote from Max Lucado: "I love you, God. I need you; So do they. Thank you." That pretty much sums it up for me, God. I love you so much, and I definitely need you, but so do they. I will continue to plant seeds as you lead me, Lord, and I will try to be sensitive to your voice today as I plant the seeds that may bear fruit in someone's life tomorrow. This has been one of my favorite conversations, God. Thank you for meeting with me again.

GOD. *It has been my pleasure. I love you, Kathy. I need you. So do they.*

KATHY. Wow! Thank you for that, God! Thank you. Love, Kathy.

Reflection of Today's Conversation

_____

_____

_____

_____

_____

_____

Scripture Application

- Jesus often used parables to help people understand his message. The enemies of Jesus were always trying to catch him saying something they could use against him. It would be very difficult to arrest someone for telling innocent stories. This was a very effective strategy.

- When Jesus spoke in parables, he explained them only to his disciples, but those who rejected his message were left in spiritual blindness and were left to wonder about their meaning. The disciples had been given the gift of the Holy Spirit which enabled them to discern the meaning of the parable. If you are a true believer, you have also been given that gift. Read *1 Corinthians 2:14, Matthew 13:10–17*, and *John 16:13* to confirm this statement.

- Jesus took advantage of occasions when multitudes would gather to hear him speak. Matthew 5:6 says, "Blessed are those who hunger for righteousness, for they shall be satisfied." People who were hungry for the word of God found what they were looking for when they gathered at the feet of Jesus and had ears to hear.

- The parable of the Sower illustrates how the seed of God's word grows and bears fruit in good hearts. Read *Matthew 13:1–9*. What do you think he meant in verse 9? Some people listen to the word of God, and in doing so, they hear and understand truth. Others block their ears to God's voice. Jesus challenged these people by making them think as the parables were being spoken.

- Read *Matthew 13:18–23*. List what each type of soil represents from the scriptures. As you think about the different types of soil Jesus used to describe the hearts of men, take a moment to evaluate your heart. What is your soil type? Could it use some fertilizer?

Wrap It Up

Great truths were spoken in very few words as Jesus conveyed his parables to the multitude as well as his disciples. It has been said that Jesus used earthly stories to teach heavenly truths. Hopefully, this parable spoke to you today. Take time to explore the many parables Jesus told in the book of Matthew. See if you have ears to hear the things God has to say. See if the Word will be planted on good soil.

- Discussion
- Closing prayer

Father,

Thank you for the parables. Thank you for giving us your Holy Spirit so that we may not only hear these words, but we may understand the true meaning of them as well. Teach us to be seed planters. Give us opportunities to plant seeds of truth, but may we understand from this conversation that although we may plant the seed, it is you who will make it grow.

Amen

So, neither he who plants nor he who waters is anything, but only God who gives growth.

—1 Corinthians 3:7

Seed Planter

Seeds come in all shapes and sizes.
They hold a mystery deep down inside.
Once planted in soil rich in goodness,
The fruit from within cannot hide.
Have you ever planted a seed;
A tomato, a squash, or a pea?
A flower, a shrub, an indoor plant,
Or maybe a beautiful tree?
Did you know you have seeds that are hidden;
Down deep in the depths of your heart?
If you ask God to guide and direct you,
Then his wisdom unto you he'll impart.
God will reveal these wonderful treasures,
Some are big, some heavy, some small.
He will show you right where to plant them.
You just need to follow, that's all.
Seeds of doubt, sadness, and worry,
Are too heavy to carry around.
So, sprinkle those by the wayside,
For you do not want those to be found.
Seeds of division and seeds of gloom,
All lead to a place of despair.
As soon as these seeds are planted,

No fruit will be found anywhere.
So, plant some seeds of love and hope,
Indeed, it's a much lighter load.
Keep watch over those who may need them,
As you travel the broken road.
Once the heart of a person is fertile,
Plant the seed with a touch and a smile.
Wait on the Lord, he will make it grow,
Though it may take a little while.
A life will be changed and fruit will be plenty,
And God will reward you that day.
Reach into your heart, keep planting those seeds,
Wait on God, he will show you the way.

Kathy M. Crouch

CHAPTER 14

COINCIDENCES

- Revelation 22:13 ESV: "*I am the Alpha and the Omega, the first and the last, the beginning and the end.*"
- Philippians 2:13 ESV: "*For it is God who works in you, both to will and to work for his good pleasure.*"
- Exodus 9:16 ESV: "*But for this purpose I have raised you up, to show you my power, and that my name may be proclaimed in all the earth.*"
- Luke 12:7 ESV: "*Why, even the hairs on your head are numbered. Fear not; you are of more value than many sparrows.*"
- Romans 8:28 ESV: "*All things work together for good for those who are called according to my purpose.*"

Let's Get Started

1. What are your thoughts concerning coincidences? Can you think of a time when something happened and you felt like it was just too strange to be a coincidence?
2. Do you ever consider the fact that a coincidence could really be the hand of God moving in your life? If so, can you give an example?

3. Can you think of times in the Old Testament where today it might be considered a coincidence, but it was actually God weaving together events for his greater purposes?
4. Do you think the still small voice of God could be connected to a coincidence?
5. Read *Revelation 22:13*. What does this tell us about God?
6. Read *Philippians 2:13*. Discuss this scripture. What does it say to you?
7. Read *Exodus 9:16*. Have you ever felt that God raised you up at a particular time and empowered you to speak the truth to someone who may have needed to hear from him?
8. Read *Luke 12:7*. How does that verse show the omniscience of our sovereign God?
9. Read *Romans 8:28*. Only God can take our mistakes and unplanned events and weave them together for his purposes. Do you think a coincidence can coexist with this verse? Why or why not?

A Conversation with God

KATHY. Dear God, it's me again.

GOD. *Yes, Kathy, what's on your mind today?*

KATHY. I have been thinking a lot lately about coincidences. Do you believe in those?

GOD. *Well, no, I don't. The world likes the idea of coincidence. It takes away any accountability to acknowledge the existence of a creator and greater purpose in their lives.*

KATHY. I'm not sure I fully understand that.

GOD. *If things just happen by chance, then your actions don't really matter. Remember, I am God. I am sovereign. I am the Alpha and the Omega—the first and the last, the beginning and the end. I am all-knowing and all-powerful. I am in control. Even before Adam and Eve brought sin into the world, I knew my son would have to die on the cross to bring redemption. I know every decision you will make and every consequence you will experience.*

KATHY. Lord, I have had so many experiences where I would think to myself there is just no way that could have happened unless you were in it somehow.

GOD. *Yes, like the day I whispered to you to choose that certain nail salon to go to?*

Exactly! It's like I felt a little nudge telling me which one to go to. The events that happened that day were so unexplainable.

GOD. *That was no coincidence, Kathy. There was someone there that day who needed to hear about me, and I used you to help make that happen. For this purpose, I have raised you up to show you my power so that my name may be proclaimed on all the earth. For you that day, it was in the salon.*

KATHY. Lord, then it must have been you who sent that worker over to talk to me. I was wondering if I had a big Jesus sign tied around my neck because he pulled his chair right up to me and began talking about you. He didn't try to hide it. He spoke with authority in a somewhat loud voice. You gave me the words to speak back to him as well. It was so strange but rewarding at the same time.

GOD. *Did you see the young girl over to the side who kept lifting her head to listen?*

KATHY. Yes, there weren't very many people in there that day, so I did notice her.

GOD. *That was no coincidence. She needed to hear about me. I gave you both the words to say, and I gave her the heart to hear and understand.*

KATHY. God, the very best part of that whole situation was when I asked him his name, and he told me it was Opie. My mind quickly went back in time, and the fondest of memories washed over me.

GOD. *Tell me more about that.*

KATHY. Now I totally understand that you worked the whole thing out. It was definitely not a coincidence! My sister was waiting on me in the car, and as I opened the door, I said, "Well, I just met Opie." She gave me a *very* strange look and then proceeded to show me what she was reading. It was an article about Mayberry. Yes, Lord—an article about Opie.

GOD. *Kathy, that was an affirmation to let you know I sent you there. I weave together all events for my greater purpose. Remember, Moses didn't just come across a burning bush. I meant to meet him there. Abraham finding a ram to sacrifice instead of his son was not a coincidence. I knew Abraham would be faithful to me so, I provided an alternative sacrifice.*

KATHY. God, I am so glad that you confirmed what I always thought to be true. I will forevermore look for those times when you are working behind the scenes to accomplish your greater goals. Albert Einstein said, "Coincidences are God's way of remaining anonymous." I really like that.

GOD. *I like that too, Kathy. Always remember how much I love you. Even the hairs on your head are numbered. Fear not, you are of more value than many sparrows. It is I who works in you both to will and to work for my good pleasure. Keep your eyes focused on me, and you will never miss an opportunity to witness my greater works and even more than that, to be a part of it. Stay focused, and be careful to listen to that still small voice. That voice will never lead you astray.*

KATHY. Thank you once again, God. You are so awesome and explain things so clearly.

GOD. *Kathy, all things work together for good for those who are called according to my purpose. You accomplished my purpose on that day. It was not a coincidence. Be sure to share our conversation with someone who might have missed an opportunity to witness my omniscient power working on their behalf to accomplish my will in their life.*

KATHY. I will do that, Lord. I actually have someone in mind. Thanks again! Love, Kathy.

Reflection of Today's Conversation

_____

_____

_____

_____

_____

_____

_____

Scripture Application

- What appears to us as random chance is in fact overseen by a sovereign God. Read *Colossians 1:16*, *Revelations 4:11*, and *Isaiah 46:9–11*. How do these verses support this statement?
- Read *Exodus 3:1–6*. Moses coming across a burning bush was not a coincidence. God met him there.
- Read *Genesis 22:1–13*. God knew Abraham would be faithful to him. It was not a coincidence that God provided an alternative sacrifice.
- Read *Luke 10:25–37*. God already knew that it was not the "righteous" of society but the disliked Samaritan who would stop and help the man.
- The word *coincidence* is translated from the Greek word *synkyrian*, which is a combination of two words: *sun* and *kurios*. *Sun* means "together with," and *kurios* means "supreme in authority." So, a biblical definition of *coincidence* would be "what occurs together by God's provincial arrangement of circumstances." What appears to us at times as random chance is, in fact, overseen by a sovereign God (Gotguestions.org podcast).

Wrap It Up

The next time something happens in your life that seems a little strange, think of it as a God incident rather than a coincidence.

Unexplained circumstances can sometimes be tools God uses to fulfill his plans. He is the sovereign creator of the universe, and it is he who works in us to will and to work his good pleasure.

- Discussion
- Closing prayer

Dear Heavenly Father,

Remind us daily that you are a sovereign God and that you are Father of all, over all, through all, and in all. You direct our steps and know every decision we will make and every consequence we will experience. Remind us that you are the creator and have a greater purpose for our lives. When something happens that we just can't explain, help us to realize that you are using these moments to reveal yourself to us and you are weaving together these events for your glory while we are here on this side of heaven.

Amen

For it is God who works in you, both to will and to work for his good pleasure.

—Philippians 2:13

Not by Chance

When strange things happen and you don't know why
An event you simply can't justify
It's not by chance
It is I
I am the first, I'll be the last
I see your future; I've seen your past

It's not by chance
It is I
I know each decision you will ever make
I guide and direct each step you'll take
It's not by chance
It is I
Because you've seen me and heard my voice
With eyes and ears, you had a choice
It's not by chance
It is I
I am the beginning, I'll be the end
Every tongue will confess, each knee will bend
It's not by chance.
It is I
Creator, sustainer, redeemer, friend
Who knows how each life on this earth will end
It's not by chance
It is I
The next time you wonder oh how could this be
Cast your eyes to the heavens and focus on me
It is not by chance that I came to save
It is not by chance there's an empty grave
It's not by chance
It is not by chance
It is I

Kathy M. Crouch

CHAPTER 15

THE BEGGAR

- John 3:16 ESV: "*For God so loved the world that he gave his only begotten son that whosoever believes in him should not perish but have eternal life.*"
- Matthew 25:40 ESV: "*Truly, I say to you, as you did it to one of the least of these my brothers, you did it to me.*"
- Hebrews 13:16 ESV: "*Do not neglect to do good and to share what you have, for such sacrifices are pleasing to God.*"

Let's Get Started

1. What comes to your mind when you are riding down the highway and at the light or stop sign, there is a person standing there holding a sign? What does the sign usually mean?
2. Have you or anyone you know ever been confronted by one of these individuals? What happened?
3. Do you consider this to be begging? If so, why? If no, why not?
4. Have you seen this happening in places other than a stoplight or intersection?
5. In our conversation today, Kathy struggles with what to do in these situations. Her heart is heavy when she sees

someone in need. What advice do you think God might give her?

6. Read *Matthew 25:40* and *Hebrews 13:16*. What do these verses say to you?

7. Read *John 3:16*. We may not sit or stand by the road with a sign in our hand, but all of us are in need of something, and our greatest need is a savior. What did God give up so that we could have eternal life and have it more abundantly?

8. What do you hope to learn in our conversation today?

A Conversation with God

KATHY. Dear God, may we talk about the beggar on the street corner? I have so many questions about this subject. When I see one of these, the question always pops in my head: what would Jesus do? I live in a small town, but lately, there seem to be more opportunities to ask that question.

GOD. *This will be a difficult conversation but one worth having.*

KATHY. I remember many years ago, I had a friend who was really struggling financially; and one day she took her little boy to get a hamburger, fries, and a soda. As they were heading back home, she came to an intersection where a man was holding a sign asking for help. Do you remember what she did God?

GOD. *Yes, she rolled down her window and gave the man her son's food.*

KATHY. When she told me that story, I cried. I thought it was such a kind and decent thing for her to do, but I knew she was very short on funds, and I felt so bad for her child. He was probably four years old, and all he saw was his delicious hamburger go out the window. How did she explain that act of kindness to him?

GOD. *Kathy, when my love abides in one's heart, it speaks to people in different ways. Your friend was one of those people who knew that no matter what her circumstances were, she could trust in the fact that I would supply her every need. Giving that food away to someone who looked hungry was easy for her because she knew her little boy would not go hungry. She used that opportunity to teach her son*

*about compassion and what it means to give to those whose needs
are greater than our own.*

KATHY. She told me that very thing. As she explained how you clearly
told her to give it away, the smile on her face showed anything
but regret. She was truly blessed by this. Please, Lord, what are
some words of wisdom you can give to me as I struggle with
giving money to those who may use it just to fund an addic-
tion instead of feeding themselves or paying a bill. I have been
approached many times as I was leaving a grocery store, and
my response has always been, "I can't give you money, but I
will pray for you." I always leave feeling like I have let someone
down. It is a terrible feeling, but I really don't know what you
want me to do in these situations.

GOD. *Did you pray for this person after you said you would?*

KATHY. Well, not as I should have. I think I was more annoyed by it
than anything else.

GOD. *It is very hard to know what to do in these circumstances. Choices
were made that led them down that path. Because you do not know
the life story of these individuals, it is hard to know what to do for
them. If one is holding a sign at a traffic light, because the light
changes so often, they do not wish to have a conversation with you;
handouts are their goal. If you have the opportunity to talk to them
as you did in the parking lot of the grocery store, just take that
opportunity to show compassion. Look them in the eye, and let them
see that you care. You are responsible to me for your loving response,
not their response to you. Pray for them; better yet, pray over them
at that very moment. That will take courage, but I will equip you.
Tell them that I love them and that my son can give them a better
life. Be that seed planter that we talked about earlier, and I will
do what it takes to make those seeds grow. Seek my will in times
like these, and I will let you know when to give and when to be
cautious.*

KATHY. My heart really goes out to them, Lord. You have blessed me
with the essentials of life, and I cannot imagine what it would
feel like to, for whatever reason, have to sit by the road with a
sign just to survive. I know there are organizations in our com-

munity that provide assistance to them, and I certainly could be more involved in that ministry.

GOD. *That is a great idea, but there is one more thing I would like for you to think about. Consider all of humanity as beggars. All men are in desperate need—maybe not a need that would cause them to sit by the road with a sign but a need greater than that. For it was I who loved the world so much that I gave my only begotten son, that whosoever would believe in him would not perish but have eternal life. I gave up something very precious to me. I showed compassion, mercy, and love to a fallen world. I am just asking you to do the same. Truly I say unto you as you do it to one of the least of these, you do it to me.*

KATHY. I must confess I have never even looked at it that way. Thank you for reminding me of just how needy we all are. Our greatest need and the greatest need of the beggar is eternal life which can only be found through your Son, Jesus. This is not our home nor their home. You have something much better awaiting us.

GOD. *Kathy, there will always be situations and opportunities to help others. People in need may not always be sitting by the street. Be sensitive to my voice when you feel the tug to give. I will tell you what to do. Do not neglect to do good and to share what you have, for such sacrifices are pleasing to me. Remember the love you have shown to people living in Nicaragua and Swaziland. You may never see the fruit this side of heaven, but just know this—I see it.*

KATHY. I can never thank you enough for allowing our paths to cross theirs. It brings great joy to know they might have a better life as we share with them the gifts you have blessed us with. I love what Ann Frank once said: "No one has ever become poor by giving." That sums it all up for me. I praise you, Lord, for taking the time to show me new things that I would have never known apart from you. Never again will I pass by one of these people without remembering this conversation. Thank you again! My heart is full. Love, Kathy.

Reflection of Today's Conversation

_____
_____
_____
_____
_____
_____

Scripture Application

- The greatest of all commandments is found in Luke's gospel 10:27 which says, "Love the Lord your God with all your heart and with all your soul and with all your strength and with all your mind, and love your neighbor as yourself." If we do that to the best of our ability, our lives will shine for Christ.
- The parable of the Good Samaritan is a great example of doing the right thing even if it's not popular or comfortable. Read *Luke 10:25–37*. What are your thoughts?
- In verse 36, Jesus asks the law expert which of the three was a neighbor to the man who fell into the hands of the robbers. What was the lawyer's reply? What did Jesus tell him to do?

Wrap It Up

Jesus is telling us to follow the Samaritan's example in our conduct. We should show compassion and love to those we encounter each day regardless of their religion or race. Our neighbor can be anyone we encounter even the beggar. There are many things we could do to help those in need, but their greatest need is to know Jesus Christ as their personal Lord and Savior. God reminded Kathy to pray for those less fortunate than herself and to give if she could. As followers of Christ, we should learn to give, expecting nothing in return.

Second Corinthians 9:7 says, "Each one must give as he has decided in his heart, not reluctantly or under compulsion, for God loves a cheerful giver." What does this verse mean to you? Brainstorm ways you or your church could begin a ministry to help those in need.

- Discussion
- Closing prayer

Father,

You are the giver of all things. You have blessed us with good homes, families, friends, and above all, you gave us your only begotten son so that we could have eternal life. There are people all around us who are less fortunate than ourselves for reasons we do not know. Please give us a caring heart and show us ways to reach out to those in need. May we honor you with every decision we make in this matter in the days ahead.

Amen

Truly, I say to you, as you did it to one of the least of these my brothers, you did it to me.

—Matthew 25:40

The Beggar

I went to the grocery store and what did I see?
A beggar in the parking lot looking at me.
I glanced in his direction and then I turned away,
I prayed dear God in heaven please tell me what to say.
At that very moment, God whispered in my ear,
Listen oh so carefully, I'll make this crystal clear.

He'll tell a sad, sad story once you look into his eyes,
It may be filled with truth; it may be filled with lies.
He'll ask you for some money that his story will validate,
Any amount you give him he will gladly appreciate.
Money is not the answer to help this beggar see,
The only thing he's missing is a gentle touch from me.
His greatest need cannot be bought it's absolutely free,
You must put your fears away and tell him about me.
Plant the seed right where you are and I will do the rest,
Let him know I love him as far as East is from the West.
A listening ear and compassionate heart can go a long, long way,
If he resists in any way, please know that that's okay.
Just be my feet, my hands, and voice in every circumstance,
The seeds you plant will surely grow; it will not be by chance.

Kathy M. Crouch

CHAPTER 16

LET GO AND LET GOD

- Philippians 4:6, 7 ESV: "*Do not be anxious about anything, but in everything by prayer and supplication with thanksgiving let your requests be made known to me and then my peace which passes all understanding would guard your heart and mind in Christ Jesus.*"
- 2 Timothy 1:7 ESV: "*For God gave us a spirit not of fear but of power and love and self-control.*"
- 2 Chronicles 7:14 ESV: "*If my people who are called by my name will humble themselves and pray, and seek my face, and turn from their wicked way; then I will hear from heaven, and I will forgive their sin, and will heal their land.*"

Let's Get Started

1. How do you feel about the direction our country is going in right now?
2. On a scale from 1–10, 1 being the lowest, how much time do you spend watching or listening to the news? How does it make you feel after listening to it?
3. Do you know of anyone who used to watch the news but has stopped for whatever reason? If so, why did they make the decision to stop?

4. In our conversation today, Kathy became anxious each time she watched the news. Read *Philippians 4:6, 7* to see what God told her about being anxious. What is the remedy? What is the reward?

5. We have been learning about being still and hearing God's voice through all the noise. Read *2 Timothy 1:7*. What part of this verse do we have to possess in order to make good decisions as to what we listen to each day?

6. How much time would you say you spend in prayer for our country and our leaders? Read *2 Chronicles 7:14* to discover the promise from God if we will do this. What are your thoughts?

A Conversation with God

KATHY. Dear God, today I would like to talk to you about the things that are going on in this country. As you know, I used to be addicted to the news. I would find the most conservative station and try to gather as much information as possible while spending three or more hours a day listening to men and women tell me how corrupt our government is, watching cities burn, watching the anchors argue with one another, and I could go on and on. I felt exhausted and horrible at the end of the night, but I would make sure I was there again at the same time every single evening.

GOD. *I saw your struggle, and believe me, you are not alone. Millions of people have been captured by the media, and the damage it does to the mind can sometimes be relentless. Let's talk about how I have helped you move forward.*

KATHY. Several weeks ago, my brother told me that he hadn't watched the news in several months. He said if our country came under attack, he would not know it, and I thought that was the craziest thing I had ever heard. How dare he not be informed!

GOD. *Yes, you were being a little judgmental, weren't you, Kathy?*

KATHY. I was not only judging; I was a little angry. I thought how could anyone with a brain not want to know what is going on in the world? I stayed strong, though, and didn't share my opinion with him. Please forgive me for the judging part.

GOD. *You're forgiven… I like the path you are on at the moment if you would like to talk about that.*

KATHY. When I began having these conversations with you, something happened. I have come to realize that there is not one single thing I can do to stop the madness. I understand that you are in total control of everything. Having people on a TV screen whom I don't even know fill my head with doom and gloom was not healthy, and it always left me feeling anxious at the end of the day. Since the day I turned it off, I have experienced so much more joy and peace. Now I get what my brother was trying to tell me.

GOD. *Yes, and as you realized this, I began to hear from you more, and your prayers began to carry a lot of weight. I saw the tears and knew you needed a touch from my hand. I told you not to be anxious about anything, but in everything, by prayer and supplication, with thanksgiving, let your requests be made known to me; and then my peace, which passes all understanding, would guard your heart and mind in Christ Jesus. You listened, and that is when you began to let go and let me carry the burdens of this world so you wouldn't have to.*

KATHY. Lord, Corrie Ten Boom said, "Worry does not empty tomorrow of its sorrow; it empties today of its strength." I have read that quote so many times and only now does it really speak to me. My strength was slowly slipping away day by day, and I didn't know why.

GOD. *Kathy, I have given you a spirit not of fear but of power and love and self-control. It takes self-control to fight this battle. When you began to trust me more and began to understand this, it was easy to stop listening to what the world had to say and concentrate more on my voice. Remember, we have been working on that part for quite some time.*

KATHY. Yes, we sure have. Since I turned off the news, I have been able to hear your voice like never before. God, our forefathers loved you, they loved this country, and they knew that this country would only stay great if it remained one nation under your great name. If they were alive today and could see how far we have fallen as a nation, they would be appalled. They would not recognize any of it.

GOD. *No, they would not. You must remember, every illness, every act of violence, every tragedy that happens in the world today can be traced back to that first encounter between the first human beings and Satan. Nothing has ever changed and will not change until I return. Satan is still on the prowl, and his ultimate goal is to destroy anything that is good. I would like to leave you with the words from 2 Chronicles 7:14 which says, "If my people who are called by my name will humble themselves and pray, and seek my face, and turn from their wicked way; then I will hear from heaven, and I will forgive their sin, and will heal their land."*

KATHY. I love those words and will etch them on my heart. It is my solemn prayer today that your children across this country will be on their knees each and every day, calling upon your name, starting with me. You did not say you might heal our land; you said you would! Our pastor told us that until we get tired of this world, we will never long for the one you have prepared for us. He is so right, so I close our conversation with these words: Even so, come, Lord Jesus! May I be found faithful when that day finally comes! I love you, Lord. Kathy.

Reflection of Today's Conversation

_____

_____

_____

_____

_____

_____

Scripture Application

- Dwight D. Moody said, "Let God have your life. He can do more with it than you can." That quote seems to coincide with Proverbs 16:3 which says, "Commit your work to the Lord, and your plans will be established." It doesn't say "might be"; it says "will be." What are your thoughts?
- Some of the best examples in the Bible that shows God's provision for his people is found in Exodus. Chapter 14 captures the Israelites' crossing of the Red Sea. God used Moses to save them from the Egyptians. When the Israelites saw the great power that the Lord had used against the Egyptians, they feared and trusted him.
- The Israelites constantly grumbled and focused on their physical needs as they were traveling through the desert, but God was focused on their need to trust him in every circumstance. Read *Exodus 15:22–27* and discuss their grumbling and how God tested their loyalty to him.
- Read *Exodus chapter 16* to find out how God sustained, tested, and encouraged the people throughout the journey in a perfect way. Be prepared to list all the things he provided.

Wrap It Up

Whatever we do while we are travelers on this earth, we must remember, we do it by the power of God and not through our own strength. We may be worried and concerned about the direction our country is going in, but we must believe that God is in total control, and we must learn to surrender all of our anxieties to him. First Peter 5:7 says, "Casting all your cares upon him for he cares for you." Exodus 14:14 brings it all together: "The Lord will fight for you, and you have only to be silent." What a promise from our Lord and Savior!

- Discussion

- Closing prayer

Father,

   We are living in trying times, but you never told us it would be easy. We humbly come before the throne of grace, asking for your love and protection all across this great country. We pray for a great awakening and a great revival among your people. Forgive us for grumbling more than we should and for not trusting you in every area of our lives. Draw us ever so close to you in the days ahead, and may everything we do bring glory and honor to your great name.

Amen

If my people who are called by my name will humble themselves and pray, and seek my face, and turn from their wicked way; then I will hear from heaven, and I will forgive their sin, and will heal their land.

—2 Chronicles 7:14

A Prayer for Our Country

We humbly pray for the US of A,
It lost its way the other day.
The other day, as strange as that appears;
To God, one day could be a thousand years.
Dear Father in Heaven, we're divided and lost,
We have pushed you aside no matter the cost.
So, we ask for your blessings, your mercy, your grace,
It's our grandchildren God, who'll be stuck in this place.
We pray for them now, for we do love them so,
And it saddens us to think this is all they may know.

May your spirit rain down Lord, all over this land,
And unite us again with the touch of your hand.
May your people now realize the importance of prayer,
And know you are listening and know that you care.
May we stay on our knees and lift up our voice,
And understand clearly there's no other choice.
We need an awakening, a revival it's true,
But what we need more is a real glimpse of you.
As you touch the heart of each woman and man,
Oh God, please bless this great country again.
We praise you and thank you for what you will do,
Lord, our prayer is to find our way back to you.
Amen

Kathy M. Crouch

CHAPTER 17

CONTINUED PRAYER

- John 14:6 ESV: "*I am the way, and the truth, and the life. No one comes to the Father except through me.*"
- 2 Peter 3:9 ESV: "*The Lord is not slow to fulfill his promise as some count slowness, but is patient toward you, not wishing that any should perish, but that all should come to repentance.*"
- James 5:16 ESV: "*The prayer of a righteous person has great power as it is working.*"
- Ephesians 3:20 ESV: "*Now to him who is able to do far more abundantly than all that we ask or think according to the power at work within us.*"

Let's Get Started

1. In today's conversation, Kathy begins her conversation with this quote by L. B. Cowman: "Pray until what you pray for has been accomplished or until you have complete assurance in your heart that it will be. Only when one of these two conditions has been met is it safe to stop persisting in prayer." Then she asks God what his thoughts are concerning this quote. What do you think God says? What would you say?

2. Do you ever pray about something for so long, day after day, that you feel like God is tired of hearing from you? Why or why not?

3. What concerns you the most and keeps you on your knees in constant prayer?

4. Kathy's greatest concern is for the lost. Read *John 14:6* and *2 Peter 3:9* to discover why praying for those who have not put their faith in Jesus Christ is of the utmost importance. What are your thoughts?

5. Read *James 5:16* and *Ephesians 3:20*. What do these two verses say to you about continued prayer? Have you ever thought that there is power inside of you to make a difference in the lives of others? Where does that power come from?

6. God sheds light on how important and powerful our prayers are in our conversation today. Find out when and if it is safe to stop petitioning.

A Conversation with God

KATHY. Dear God, I would like to begin our conversation today with one of my very favorite quotes from L. B. Cowman. It says, "Pray until what you pray for has been accomplished or until you have complete assurance in your heart that it will be. Only when one of these two conditions has been met is it safe to stop persisting in prayer." What do you think about that, God?

GOD. *I must say that I do agree with that statement.*

KATHY. From the day I first read that, it has caused me to think about and realize how important our petitions really are. She also said, "Prayer not only is calling upon God but is also a battle with Satan."

GOD. *Yes, that is true, and Mrs. Cowman also said that because I use intersession as a mighty weapon of victory in conflict, I alone must decide when it is safe to cease from petitioning.*

KATHY. Yes, Lord, and that is where I struggle sometimes. I feel like I pray the same thing over and over again and sometimes I feel like you get tired of my constant tugging.

GOD. *I will never get annoyed or tired of your prayers. Sincere, heartfelt prayers are what connects us, and it is my desire that you find time out of each day to talk with me.*

KATHY. Lord, do you give us burdens? I feel like you have given me a heavy burden for those who are lost and have chosen not to believe in the redemption of your Son, Jesus. For the life of me, I can't understand their decision, so because they can't pray for themselves, I try to do it for them. Many times, this same prayer has continued for years. It is so easy to give up after such a long time because I can only see today. I would be devastated if one of these souls were to leave this earth without knowing your Son. What am I to do, God?

GOD. *You continue, Kathy. Your prayers are powerful. Because I gave men a choice, some have hardened their hearts toward my Son. The enemy has convinced many people that I don't exist or that they can get along just fine in this world without me. I want to use my children as vessels to help bring more people into the kingdom.*

KATHY. Lord, when I think about how narrow that path to life is in Matthew's gospel, I shudder to think about how few people will find it. You clearly tell us all that we are sinners and in need of a Savior. You tell us that you are the way, the truth, and the life; no man comes to you but through your Son, Jesus. I understand that, and it's so easy. Why can't they just get it?

GOD. *Kathy, it all began in the garden. Choice can be good or bad. I have been rejected throughout the ages; however, I am not slow to fulfill my promises, as some count slowness, but patient toward you, not wishing that any should perish but that all should reach repentance. It is still a choice. All of your prayers have been heard. You may not know what I am doing at this very moment in each of their lives, but don't you ever stop lifting them up to me. They need you, and they need me.*

KATHY. God, I humbly come before you, thanking you for those times when you laid it upon my heart to go pray with my brothers. They both had different needs at particular times in their lives, and I felt your tug to go each time to pray with them. I had no idea what I was going to say, but you equipped me on both occasions. I can see the fruit of both visits. I guess that is another way you reach hearts. You equip your children to be your hands, feet, and voice.

GOD. *You were obedient, and those prayers gave me opportunities to do great work. "The prayer of a righteous person has great power as it is working." Remember, whether you are praying alone or with someone, I am always there in your midst, and I hear your petitions. Learn to expect the unexpected in times like these because I am able to do far more abundantly, more than all that you ask or think, according to the power at work within you. That power within you comes from the Holy Spirit, and your faith in me is what takes you to your knees to release that power within you. How are you feeling right now?*

KATHY. I feel like I have been rambling through this conversation. So much has been said, and I am trying to put it all together.

GOD. *Well, let me see if I can help pull it all together for you. Just stay on your knees, share the good news of redemption every chance you get, and know that I hear your prayers. I may be waiting for the perfect moment when I can intercede most effectively in one of those precious souls you are praying for.*

KATHY. Lord, I will end with this prayer that I wrote months ago:

Dear God,

Let me know when it is safe to cease petitioning. I will continue to pray until I receive the assurance that my prayer has been answered. Truly I will wait upon you.

Love,
Kathy

Reflection of Today's Conversation

_____

_____

_____

_____

_____

_____

Scripture Application

- God often used parables to convey his messages. Today we will look at two of those parables as we dig a little deeper into persistent prayer.
- Read *Luke 11:5–13*. The man who repeatedly knocks on his friend's door receives what he asked for because he was persistent, not because of the friendship. God goes on to say if we ask, seek, and knock, we will receive. *Don't give up! Never stop praying!*
- Read *Luke 18:1–8.* The purpose of this parable is to encourage us as Christians to always pray and never lose heart. If the unjust judge would do the right thing for this widow, surely God, who is just, will do the same for us. We must continue in faith knowing that God hears our prayers. Verse 8 should give us a clear vision of the importance of persistent prayer as Jesus wonders if he will find faith here when he returns. *Don't give up! Never stop praying!*
- Charles Spurgeon said, "We must pray to pray and continue in prayer so that our prayers may continue." Such few words with so much meaning!

Wrap It Up

Prayer is essential to the Christian life. God says in 1 John 5:14 "And this is the confidence that we have toward him, that if we ask anything according to his will, he hears us." Kathy was concerned for the lost, and God assured her that it was not his will that any should perish but that all should reach repentance. God hears us when we pray, and because his ways are not our ways and his time is not our time, persist in prayer, knowing that he is working behind the scenes and he will intervene at the perfect time, then we can then give him the glory and honor for what he has done.

- Discussion
- Closing prayer

Father,

What an awesome God we serve. Thank you that you hear us when we pray. Teach us to stay focused and to continue to lift our petitions up to you daily. May we never think for a moment that you will not move on our behalf. When you are silent, help us to understand that it's all about your will being done in every situation. May your will be done on earth as it is in heaven, Lord, and may you find us faithful on your great return.

Amen

The Lord is not slow to fulfill his promise as some count slowness, but is patient toward you, not wishing that any should perish, but that all should reach repentance.

—2 Peter 3:9

The Lost

My heart is heavy
So today I pray for the lost
Today I pray for those
Who can not

Will not
Pray for themselves
Touch them today, Lord
In such a way
That they feel your hand
Mighty on their shoulder
In such a way
That they
Begin to lose themselves
To search for something higher
Break every stronghold
That keeps them from
Searching for you
Close every opportunity
Until they see their need
For saving grace
Until they see their need
To seek your face
Humble them Lord
Bring them to their knees
Please I pray
Do it today
To God be the glory
Amen

Kathy M. Crouch

CHAPTER 18

SEASONS

- Ecclesiastes 3:1 ESV: "*For everything there is a season, and a time for every matter under heaven.*"
- Proverbs 16:9 ESV: "*In their hearts, humans plan their course, but the Lord establishes his steps.*"
- Proverbs 3:5, 6 ESV: "*Trust in the Lord with all your heart, do not lean on your own understanding. In all your ways acknowledge him, and he will make straight your paths.*"
- Jeremiah 29:11 ESV: "*For I know the plans I have for you declares the Lord, plans for welfare and not for evil, to give you a future and a hope.*"
- Psalm 61: 1, 2 ESV: "*Hear my cry oh God, listen to my prayer; from the end of the earth, I will call to you. When my heart is faint, lead me to the rock that is higher than I.*"

Let's Get Started

1. God so graciously gave us four seasons of the year: spring, summer, fall, and winter. Do you have a favorite season? What makes it so special?
2. Read *Ecclesiastes 3:1*. God refers to seasons in a much different way in this verse. What are your thoughts here?

3. Seasons may be filled with joy and others disappointment. Why do you think God allows us to experience these different seasons?

4. Many of us find ourselves experiencing different seasons according to the events going on in our lives. Are you in a particular season right now?

5. Read *Proverbs 3:5, 6.* What does this verse say to you? What often happens when we try to figure it all out on our own? What does it mean to "acknowledge him?"

6. Read *Jeremiah 29:11.* What comfort does this verse bring you when you consider all of the obstacles that may lie ahead as you forge on into the future?

7. Read *Proverbs 16:9.* Think about the desires of your heart and your steps going forward. What part of this verse gives you hope that everything will turn out okay?

8. Read *Psalm 61: 1, 2.* In the conversation we will read today, Kathy ends with this verse as a prayer in which she prays often. How can this verse bring comfort to you when you find yourself in a difficult season?

A Conversation with God

KATHY. Good morning God. It's raining again. You have sent a lot of that our way lately.

GOD. *Yes, you will need this when summer rolls around and the days are hot and dry.*

KATHY. Yes, I know. You are always looking out for us, and sometimes we can only see the clouds. I guess we should really be looking for the rainbow.

GOD. *So, did you have anything other than the rain on your mind today?*

KATHY. Well, there are several things on my mind this morning, but the thing that weighs heavily on my heart is this season that I am in. Since the pandemic came upon us and life changed, as we knew it, I keep thinking about the scripture in Ecclesiastes that says, "For everything there is a season, and a time for every matter under heaven."

GOD. *Kathy, the very first thing I had to think about before I created it all was time. I had to fit everything inside of that. I am the one who creates each moment of time. Each season has its appropriate time in the cycle of life.*

KATHY. Lord, I think about the cycle I was in before everything changed. I was busy, Lord, so busy. After I retired from teaching, you filled my life with so many rewarding opportunities, and that season of my life was fun, and you surrounded me with so many friends—new friends and friends from the past. Then it's like you snapped your fingers, and it all vanished.

GOD. *Yes, seasons always change. Nothing stays the same forever. Some seasons may be filled with joy and excitement while others may bring disappointment and sorrow. In these times, I need for you to submit to my plans and trust in my purposes for your life.*

KATHY. I must confess, Lord, I don't think I would be having these conversations with you had things stayed the same.

GOD. *We may have talked, but you may have been too busy to write them down.*

KATHY. I was way too busy to sit down with pen and paper. I had places to go, people to see, and things to do. I have learned something about friendships and family during this season, God. I think you give friends to us along with the moments so that we can learn and grow during that particular season. I have now realized that family is to be cherished and never taken for granted.

GOD. *You are right, Kathy. Seasons were created to help you grow and to maybe see things differently. You are in a quiet season now because I needed to show you what is important and what really doesn't matter right now. Always remember, in their hearts, humans plan their course, but it is I that establishes their steps. You are in the season that I planned for you. It is a perfect plan for your life. Trust me, and know that when the rain stops, there will be another season and another door that I will open for you. Carefully enter in, and you will see me on the other side.*

KATHY. That brings me so much comfort, Lord. One of my favorite scriptures is Proverbs 3:5, 6 where you tell us to lean not unto our own understanding but in all our ways acknowledge you and you will direct our paths. I confess that I don't understand everything that comes my way, but as long as I know who holds my hand, the next season will be one of hope filled with lots of sun.

GOD. *I promise that I have good plans for you, Kathy, plans for welfare and not for evil, to give you a future and a hope. I will direct your path each and every day if you will let me.*

KATHY. I would like that very much. I will close our conversation today with a prayer from one of the Psalms. I pray it often, and it brings such joy to my heart. Psalm 61:1, 2: "Hear my cry oh God, listen to my prayer. From the end of the earth, I will call to you. When my heart is faint, lead me to the rock that is higher than I." That rock is you, Jesus. Whatever season I find myself in, if it leads me to that particular rock, everything will turn out just fine! I love you and praise you. Kathy.

Reflection of Today's Conversation

_____

_____

_____

_____

_____

_____

Scripture Application

- "When you accept the fact that sometimes seasons are dry and times are hard and that God is in control of both, you will discover a sense of divine refuge, because the hope then is in God and not in yourself" (Charles R. Swindoll). What are your thoughts after reading this quote?
- God is sovereign. He knows the number of hairs on our heads. He has scheduled each day of our lives. He already knows the seasons we will go through. Nothing catches

him by surprise. Everything that happens in our life is for his glory and for our good. Read *Psalm 135:6* to remind us that he is in control and does what he pleases in all heaven and earth.

- God told Kathy in the conversation that before anything was created, he created time and then had to fit everything inside of that. Solomon reminds us in *Ecclesiastes 3:1–8* that there are things in this world beyond our control. Read these verses, and revel in the fact that God, in his sovereignty, created a time for every single thing under heaven.

Wrap It Up

Ecclesiastes 3:11 sums up this lesson: "He has made everything beautiful in its time. Also, he has put eternity into man's heart, yet so that he cannot find out what God has done from the beginning to the end." We will never understand exactly why God does what he does or why, but we must trust him to have all knowledge and trust that he will reveal to us what we need to know at the perfect time. He is a good and faithful God. No matter what season we find ourselves in, we must realize that God knew we would be there before we did. To God be the glory!

- Discussion
- Closing prayer

Father,

We know that everything under heaven is under your authority. Help us to seek your face not only during the difficult seasons of life but also in the seasons of joy and peace. In the days and weeks ahead, may we learn to never lean on our own understanding, but in all our ways acknowledge you so that you may direct our path.

Amen

For everything there is a season, and a time
for every matter under heaven.

—Ecclesiastes 3:1

Seasons

Are you in a season of doubt or shame?
Call out to Jesus, call him by name.
Are your days uncertain, afraid of tomorrow?
Give your troubles to God, release all your sorrow.
Do not walk through the valley,
Do not walk it alone,
Cry out to Jesus till your fears are all gone.
Today may look dreary and all may seem lost,
But Jesus went to Calvary, he knew well the cost.
He went there for you; he went there for me,
For your sins and mine, he died on that tree.
Nothing's too hard for him to achieve.
All he requires is for us to believe.
No matter the season you find yourself in,
Fall on your knees, cry out, and then…
All things will be brighter than the day before;
Your season of sadness shall be no more.
Because he's the healer of a broken heart,
Trusting in him is where it must start.
Fall on your knees and fervently pray,
Cast all your cares upon Jesus today.

Kathy M. Crouch

CHAPTER 19

ASSEMBLING TOGETHER

- Psalm 117: 1–2 ESV: "*All ye nations praise the Lord. All ye people, praise him because the Lord loves us very much, and his truth is everlasting.*"
- Luke 11:9 ESV: "*And I tell you, ask and it will be given to you, seek, and you will find, knock, and it will be opened to you.*"
- Ephesians 4:11, 12 ESV: "*And he gave the apostles, the prophets, the evangelists, the shepherds, and teachers to equip the saints for the work of ministry, for building up the body of Christ.*"
- Philippians 2:13 ESV: "*For it is I who works in you, both to will and to work for my good pleasure.*"
- Hebrews 10:25 ESV: "*Do not neglect to meet together, as it is the habit of some, but encourage one another, and all the more as you see the day drawing near.*"

Let's Get Started

1. On a scale from 1–10, 10 being the most important, how important do you feel it is to meet together as a congregation for worship service? Please explain your answer.

2. When COVID-19 fell upon our community and we could not meet together, what were some of your feelings then, and what are your feelings now that we are back together again?

3. Read *Psalm 117*. The psalmist encourages all of us to praise the Lord. What would you like to praise God for today?

4. Read *Luke 11:9*. Kathy is thanking God for talking with her through these conversations and never wants to take it for granted. What does he say to reassure her that she always has his ear?

5. Do you feel like God used the pandemic to change the lives of people in your church? Do you think God wants your church to go back to the way it was before the pandemic? Why or why not? What were some of the changes in your church during this time?

6. Read *Philippians 2:13* and *Ephesians 4: 11–12*. What do these verses say about the way God designed his church?

7. Read *Hebrews 10:25*. What is God encouraging us to do as Christians as we wait for his return?

A Conversation with God

KATHY. Dear God, I love Psalm 117 which says, "All ye nations praise the Lord. All ye people, praise him because the Lord loves us very much, and his truth is everlasting. Praise the Lord." I would like to begin our conversation this morning just praising you and thanking you for another day to hear your voice. May I never take these moments for granted.

GOD. *I delight in our conversations, Kathy. Keep on asking, and it will be given to you. Seek, and you will find. Knock, and it will be opened to you. What is on your mind today?*

KATHY. My husband often uses this analogy to describe how important it is for your church to assemble together. He tells us to imagine a grill full of charcoal that has been burning for a while. The flames have died down, and there is a soft glow of white embers. The charcoal is so hot you can feel the heat from a distance. Then he poses this question: What would happen if you took one piece of that charcoal out and set it off to the side by itself? The obvious answer is it would eventually burn out.

GOD. *That is a perfect way to describe what happens when just one or more of my children fall away from the church.*

KATHY. Yesterday, as I took my seat on the pew, I was quickly reminded of how precious and important the assembling together of people of like faith really is. It has been a year since the pandemic hit our country, and our church was forced to go through many changes during that time. For a short time, I felt like I was that piece of charcoal as we could not meet together at all. Our pastor and deacons kept it all together by diligently seeking your face and asking for your guidance. Every need we had was met by you, and now things seem to be getting back to the way it was before.

GOD. *You are going to learn much today through this conversation. If you remember, it was in our first talk that I told you it was I who allowed this all to take place. Sometimes my people get a little too comfortable with the status quo. Sometimes I have to shake things up to wake things up. It is not my will for your church to get back to the way it was before.*

KATHY. Oh my! This is going to be a very interesting conversation. In my devotion this morning, Paul David Tripp said, "Corporate worship is designed to once again clear up our confusion as to what is truly important in life." Maybe it takes this kind of change to show us humans what really matters.

GOD. *Yes, that is true. There are many things you may discover that I did in the lives of the people in your church during this past year—things that would have never occurred otherwise. Going back to the way it was before the pandemic is not an option. I am preparing many of you for greater things.*

KATHY. Lord, you know I am a devotional and quote girl. This makes me think of the quote by Rebecca Barlow Jordan, who said, "God is more interested in changing us than in changing our circumstances though sometimes he does both." Wow! That really speaks to me as to what you are doing in and through our church family.

GOD. *I designed you for corporate worship. It is when you are together that you draw strength from one another. You encourage one another. This is where you hear my word spoken, and I have blessed you with a pastor who only speaks the truth. You bring glory and honor to me as you worship through psalms, songs, prayers, and praise.*

KATHY. Paul explained in the book of Ephesians that the church is designed by you, God, as he says, "And he gave the apostles, the prophets, the evangelists, the shepherds, and teachers to equip the saints for the work of ministry, for building up the body of Christ."

GOD. *Yes, and as I said earlier, I am doing great and mighty works in the members of your church. For it is I who works in you, both to will and to work for my good pleasure. It is I who will benefit from all of the changes you have gone through this past year. Do you think we would have been having these conversations if things had stayed the same?*

KATHY. I really doubt it, God. I had to learn to be still and hear your voice. That is a lesson so very hard to learn apart from your spirit drawing me closer day by day. I thank you and praise you for it! Thank you for blessing our church for so many years and for the sweet spirit that is there each time the door opens. We all feel it! I look forward to seeing all of the great things you have in store for us.

GOD. *Do not neglect to meet together, as it is the habit of some, but encourage one another, and all the more as you see the day drawing near.*

KATHY. Thank you, Lord! It is my earnest prayer that our congregation will stay united and never take our assembling together for granted. Love, Kathy.

Reflection of Today's Conversation

_____

_____

_____

_____

_____

_____

Scripture Application

- During the COVID-19 pandemic, the church got a glimpse of how quickly its freedoms can be taken away. The church is not a building; it is the assembling together of God's people. We were told that we could not assemble together, and that caused many people to realize how the freedom of worship should not be taken for granted. God designed us for corporate worship.

- There are many benefits we receive from worshipping together, but the one thing that holds the church together is prayer. Matthew 18:20 says, "For where two or more are gathered in my name, there am I among them." Two or more have great significance. There is power in numbers. Today we will read about the events that happened in the book of Acts. Chapter 5 tells us that all the apostles were imprisoned. This, of course, did not stop them from preaching the good news. After James is beheaded for his faith and the church hears the news, the people become real concerned when they realize the same fate may be waiting for Peter.

- Read *Acts 12:4, 5*. We find here that earnest prayer was made for Peter by the church. How would you define *earnest prayer*? Have there been moments in your life when you earnestly prayed for something or someone? Did the "earnest" part seem to make a difference in the outcome?

- Read *Acts 12:6–11*. Why do you think Peter was sleeping peacefully the night before he is to be executed? When the angel appeared, Peter thought he was seeing a vision. At what moment, did Peter realize that this was truly divine intervention?

- Read *Acts 12:12–17*. The people were praying, and when Peter showed up at the prayer meeting, at first, these prayer warriors did not believe that God had actually answered their prayer. They thought it was his guardian angel banging on the door. When they finally went to see for themselves, they believed that God had answered their prayers.

- The people could hardly believe their eyes when they saw Peter. They probably believed God would do what they asked, but because it was done so quickly and miraculously, their faith was not as strong as it should have been. How does this account in the book of Acts help us to understand how weak our faith can be at times? What does this reveal to us about the importance of assembling together as a body of believers?

Wrap It Up

Earnest prayer to God was made for Peter by the church. Peter was released from prison by the hand of God. Assembling together in prayer and believing is what made the difference. As believers, we need to meet together, pray together, worship together, encourage one another and bear one another's burdens. We should never take the assembling together for granted because the events that happened during the pandemic could easily happen again.

- Discussion
- Closing prayer

Father,

Thank you for reminding us through Scripture as well as current events how precious and important it is for your children to gather together. May we understand how very precious this gathering really is. You remind us in your Word that the gates of hell shall not prevail against your church. Pour out your Spirit among your people, Lord, and even more so as we see the day coming of your great return.

Amen

Do not neglect to meet together, as it is the habit of some, but encourage one another, and all the more as you see the day drawing near.

—Hebrews 10:25

Assembling Together

I think I'll go to church today; I heard my mama say,
I'll join the congregation, as they worship, sing, and pray.
I think I'll just stay home today; I heard my daddy boast,
I never really met the Father, Son, and Holy Ghost.
My mama took me by the hand, and out the door we went,
I did not understand exactly what my daddy meant.
The preacher told a story of a man from Galilee,
I asked my mom what does this story have to do with me?
My mom and I walked down the aisle, then down on bended knee,
I saw a tear roll down her cheek as she grabbed hold of me.
My son, you may not understand, but time will be your guide,
When God decides you're ready, you'll learn why Jesus died.
Until that time we'll come to church, we'll listen, learn and grow,
That's the only way to understand the things you need to know.
The people daddy didn't know, are they at church today?
Oh yes, my son all three are here, they hear us when we pray.
My mama tucked me in tonight, we knelt beside my bed,
I listened very carefully and this is what she said.
I come before the throne of grace, I pray you're hearing me,
God help my husband understand the blessed Trinity.
She prayed that prayer so many times, it carried so much weight,
When Sunday came my daddy said, "Come on let's don't be late!"
My mama took me by the hand, my daddy led the way,
We'll join the congregation yes, we'll worship, sing and pray.

Kathy M. Crouch

CHAPTER 20

EMPTY NEST

- Ecclesiastes 3:1 ESV: *"For everything there is a season, and a time for every matter under heaven."*
- Genesis 1:28 ESV: "Be *fruitful and multiply and fill the earth and subdue it, and have dominion over the fish of the sea and over the birds of the heavens and over everything that moves on the earth."*
- Proverbs 22:6 ESV: *"Train up a child in the way he should go; even when he is old, he will not depart from it."*
- Romans 8:28 ESV: *"All things work together for good for those who are called according to his purpose."*
- 1 John 5:14 ESV: *"Anything you ask according to his will, he hears us."*
- 1 Corinthians 13:7 ESV: "Love bears all things, believes all things, hopes all things, and endures all things."

Let's Get Started

1. Where have you heard the phrase "empty nest?" What does it bring to mind when you hear this? Have you ever experienced anything associated with an empty nest?
2. In today's conversation, Kathy needed answers to some of her struggles when it comes to this topic. She managed to

relate birds to children, and God was able to comfort her and give her answers to some of her cares and concerns. He began by reminding her to think about the truth in *Ecclesiastes 3:1*. Read and discover the comforting words of our Lord. How could this verse be connected to an empty nest?

3. What is the one thing both birds and children eventually do? Read *Genesis 1:28*. To whom was God speaking? God gave us the gift of children and the gift of birds. How could both of these be considered a gift? If you know anything about birds, what could be some things God wants to show us by watching and understanding their life cycle? What could be some things God wants parents to learn by gifting them with children?

4. Read *Proverbs 22:6, Romans 8:28, 1 John 5:14*, and *1 Corinthians 13:7*. We will find out how God uses these verses as words of comfort in context, and we will discuss them as we read the conversation.

A Conversation with God

KATHY. Dear God, springtime is upon us, and the birds are beginning to build their nests. I love waking up in the morning to their chirping sounds. Just last week, Lauren shared with me that there was a nest in her front door wreath with several eggs inside. One morning she lifted Emery up to see them, and after that, it became an everyday event where Emery and the neighborhood kids would gather around to see if any had hatched. The day finally came for one of these tiny birdies to crack out of its shell, and Em yelled with excitement, "Can we keep it? Can we put it in a cage?" Lauren had been given the task of explaining how that is not how things work. She explained how the baby birds would all hatch and fly away and that it was your plan for them to do so. That is when I knew what my next conversation would need to be.

GOD. *I was wondering when you would get to this. There are many things to talk about here. What concerns you today?*

KATHY. Lord, as I try to get my thoughts together, I think this quote by Jennifer Quinn will help guide this conversation. She said, "There are two times when parenting is the most difficult; when the first baby arrives at home, and when the adult first leaves home." Her words ring so true, and as I think about these birds leaving their nest, I have read where this whole event takes about twenty-one days. When you bless us with children, it takes years before they "fly away," but it seems like the years are but a few days. It's as though in the blink of an eye, they are gone.

GOD. *Yes, Kathy, for everything there is a season and a time for every matter under heaven.*

KATHY. Yes, Lord, and sometimes seasons can bring different emotions out in us. Our children consume our lives for so many years, and then they leave. Just as a mother bird is preparing her chicks to live a life without her, parents are doing the same thing but for much longer. I find a bird's life very interesting. Nearly all tree-nesting birds are born without flight feathers. They are naked, so to speak, with a little fuzz on their bodies, just like our little ones. For more than a month, the chicks are completely flightless and are totally dependent on their mother. When their flight feathers appear, she teaches them to fly. They are clumsy at first but soon catch on, much like when our children are learning to walk. Finally, the chicks have to learn to find their own food; then one by one, they leave. Lord, the day my children were ready to "leave the nest" was so hard for me.

GOD. *Kathy, children and birds are gifts from me. After I finished all of my creation, I told Adam and Eve to be fruitful and multiply and fill the earth and subdue it and have dominion over the fish of the sea and over the birds of the heavens and over everything that moves on the earth. That was then and is still today my perfect plan. You might say that one of the reasons I created birds was to wake you in the morning with their singing to put a smile on your face. I created children to teach you so many things. By becoming a parent, you learned how to love as you have never loved before. You acquired patience and understanding. You learned what mercy and grace really mean. You learned that it's not all about you any longer. Do you remember the most important thing I told you as you were raising your children?*

KATHY. Yes, you said to train up a child in the way he should go; even when he is old, he will not depart from it. That was always something I thought about because the most important thing parents should do is to teach their children to know you and to have a saving knowledge of your Son, Jesus. For me, the greatest gift for a mother is just knowing that her children will be with you one day. That is really all that matters. Thank you for receiving them when they asked. I just have one more thing I would like to talk to you about.

GOD. *What is that?*

KATHY. Why did two of my children have to "fly" so far away?

GOD. *I have a purpose for your children. Remember, Kathy, for those who love me, all things work together for good for those who are called according to my purpose. They are exactly where they need to be for such a time as this. I work in all things for good. They will be fine. I am always one step ahead of them, leading them in the way they should go. Know that I hear you when you pray for them. This is the confidence I leave with you. Anything you ask according to my will, I hear you. Rest in that promise as your children forge ahead with their own path. They too will learn valuable lessons from me as they prepare their own children to one day leave their nest.*

KATHY. I love our conversations, God. You always make everything so clear to me. You tell us in your Word that love bears all things, believes all things, hopes all things, and endures all things. You are that love, and that is much like the kind of love a mother has for her children. It is because of your steadfast love that I can face each day knowing that my children will be just fine on their own. Oh, and one more thing—you must really love me, God, because you gave me the most precious gift of all—grandchildren! That would be an interesting conversation for sure! Love, Kathy.

Reflection of Today's Conversation

_____

_____

_____

_____

_____

_____

Scripture Application

- I often use the phrase "It takes a village to raise a child." I believe God brings many people into our lives who help us train our children in the way they should go. I am a firm believer that it takes both a mother and a father to raise children in this immoral society we find ourselves living in. One day our precious ones will leave the nest and venture out into this world of unknowns. It is the job of parents to make sure they are grounded in God's Word before they leave.

- According to data collected by *Promise Keepers* and *Baptist Press*, if a father does not go to church even if the wife does, only one child in fifty will become a regular worshiper. If a father does go regularly, regardless of what the mother does, between two-thirds and three-quarters of their children will attend church as adults. If a father attends church irregularly, between half and two-thirds of their kids will attend church with some regularity as adults. A dad's influence on a child's faith is huge.

- Today we will read the words Moses spoke by the inspiration of the Holy Spirit to the dads of the new generation. Read *Deuteronomy 6:1–9*. Discuss the commands that God wants his servant to reveal to us when it comes to raising our children using the following:

o   Who?

_____

_____

_____

o   What?

_____

_____

_____

o   When?

_____

_____

_____

o   Where?

_____

_____

_____

o   How?

_____

_____

_____

- Read *Ephesians 6:1–4*. These verses speak to children and fathers. What might be the results if these commands are followed?
- Listen to the words of Adrian Rogers:

> Children are truly a blessing from God. Unfortunately, they don't come with an instruction manual. But there's no better place to find advice on parenting than the word of God, which reveals a Heavenly Father who loves us and calls us his children. It contains great examples of godly parents. It gives direct instructions on how to parent, and it is filled with many principles we

can apply as we strive to be the best parents we can be.

Wrap It Up

My pastor's daughter who recently married raised concerns about starting a family due to the moral decline in our country. Her father quickly said, "We need Christians to continue having children!" I must agree with him. We are the salt and the light, and if we stop bringing children into this world and Christians cease to be, how much darker will our world become? As parents, God must be the center of our lives, and our children must see our passion as we serve him each day. We must lead by example. Psalm 127:3–5 says,

> Behold, children are a heritage from the Lord, the fruit of the womb, a reward. Like in the hand of a warrior are the children of one's youth. Blessed is the man who fills his quiver with them.

- Discussion
- Closing prayer

Father,

> Thank you for children. They are precious, and we know how much you love them. Being a parent can be hard and rewarding at the same time. Help us who have children to train them up in the way they should go. Show us how to lead them, and it is our prayer that they will be Christians all the days of their lives. When our children grow up and leave the nest, give us enough grace to let them go without leaving us with a broken heart. It is in Jesus's name we pray.

Amen

Train up a child in the way he should go; even
when he is old, he will not depart from it.

—Proverbs 22:6

Did You Pass the Test?

Children…
A gift from God;
A test from God;
Did you pass?
Did you learn how to love unconditionally?
Were you patient, understanding, and kind?
Did you learn about mercy and grace?
Was it all about you?
Was it all about them?
Did you tell them about God?
How Jesus died for them; How he loves them.
Did they learn how to pray?
Did you take them to church?
Did you read to them, hug them, kiss them good night?
Children grow up fast.
You blink and it's over.
They leave the nest.
They fly away.
Some near, some far away.
God may bless them with children one day.
Will they pass the test?
Did they learn from the best?
God gave you a test…
Did you pass?

Kathy M. Crouch

CHAPTER 21

DON'T SWEAT THE SMALL STUFF

- Psalm 121:8 ESV: "*The Lord will keep your going out and your coming in from this time forth and forevermore.*"
- James 1:2, 3 ESV: "*Consider it all joy, my brothers, when you meet trials of various kinds, for you know that the testing of our faith produces steadfastness.*"
- Isaiah 41:10 ESV: "*Fear not, for I am with you; be not dismayed, for I am your God; I will strengthen you, I will help you, I will uphold you with my righteous right hand.*"
- 1 Peter 5:7 ESV: "*Casting all your anxieties on him; because he cares for you.*"
- Isaiah 40:31 ESV: "*Those who wait for the Lord shall renew their strength; they shall mount up like wings on eagles; they shall run and not grow weary; they shall walk and not faint.*"

Let's Get Started

1. What is your first thought upon reading this title? What would you consider to be small stuff? Has anything ever happened in your life that seemed to put things into perspective—important things versus not so important things?

2. In today's conversation, Kathy was able to reflect on these things after a tragic accident happened to be the tool by which God helped her to understand how fragile life is and how small things aren't really worth worrying too much about. Read *Psalm 121:8*. How could this verse have been a comfort to Kathy at this time?

3. Read *James 1:2, 3*. God has repeated this verse to Kathy so many times in so many different situations. Discuss the power in this verse. Do you consider it joy when trials come your way? How can God use trials to strengthen our faith? Have you ever thought about how strong your faith would be if there was never a trial in your life?

4. Read *Isaiah 41:10*. The words that should catch your attention are "*I am*" and "*I will*." He used *I am* twice and *I will* three times. Never did he say "I might" be or "I might" help. Put your name at the beginning of that verse, and read it again. There is so much hope found there!

5. Read *1 Peter 5:7*. God cares for us and is willing to take our cares and concerns upon himself if we will just trust him.

6. Read *Isaiah 40:31*. What do you think it means to wait for the Lord? How easy is that to do in this fast-paced world we live in?

7. Kathy learned so much through this conversation with God. Her life was never quite the same.

A Conversation with God

KATHY. Dear God, I have been surrounded by a lot of people lately who complain about the smallest of things. I have come to realize over the years that the only things that really matter to me are you, my family, my church, and my friends. The event that helped me realize just how we shouldn't sweat the small stuff was when Russell almost lost his life in the four-wheeler accident. You were in that situation from the beginning to the end.

GOD. *Yes, Kathy. I will watch over your coming and going both now and forevermore. I was indeed with Russell that day. I was there*

*before he arrived, and I knew what was about to happen, so I put
everyone in the exact place they needed to be.*

KATHY. Lord, you certainly showed us your awesome power that day.
For anyone to understand how miraculous this was, I need to
give great detail. He was on a trail in what we Carolinians like to
refer to as the middle of nowhere. Because he chose not to wear
his helmet that day, he was hurt really badly. He had been on
that trail many times before, but he had no idea that the DOT
had cut the entire hillside of dirt away and left a ten-foot drop
on the other side. As he fell, the four-wheeler landed on his face.
By your mercies and grace, he survived. I would like to list all
of the things you provided, Lord, as my way to thank you and
praise you for each blessing of that day.

- Russell was able to get up and walk out of the wooded area.
- His cousin just happened to be fishing on the land next to
  him and was able to help him call for help—definitely not
  a coincidence.
- His dad answered the phone and could hear the distress in
  his voice, so he immediately jumped in his truck, headed
  that way, and Russell was walking out of the woods. It
  would have been nearly impossible to reach him had you
  not carried him to the highway.
- My niece, who was a nurse in the trauma center of the exact
  hospital he would later be transferred to, had just arrived
  for our daughter's wedding shower and had not even had
  time to unpack her bags, so she headed right over to our
  local hospital. When the decision was made to transfer him
  to Carolinas Medical Center in Charlotte, North Carolina,
  my niece led the way; and because she was familiar with
  everything, we easily found our way, and things ran very
  smoothly.
- The surgeon on call that night was having dinner with
  friends and family. He arrived at the hospital all dressed up,
  and we began apologizing for the inconvenience, and his
  only response was, "This is what I do." We later found out

from employees there that he was an extremely competent surgeon, and we should be thankful that he was on call. He did an outstanding job of repairing Russell's sweet face. We joke about how the Dr. gave him a new dimple.

- He healed nicely, and his family and friends were so supportive. That is when his best friend since fourth grade decided the friendship would take on a whole new meaning. She is now my daughter-in-law. I bet you knew all about that too, didn't you, God?

I just want to thank you and praise you for your goodness during that whole episode. It changed everything for me. I no longer look at trials the same way after that incident. The small things that I once worried about became really, really small, and the bigger things just caused me to search for you in order to get through them. You tell us in James 1:2, 3 to "consider it all joy when you meet trials of various kinds, for you know that the testing of your faith produces steadfastness." That rings so true, Lord. I learned, as a mom who nearly lost her son, that my faith was indeed tested by fire, and I came out so much stronger on the other side. I think sometimes you just have to change things up to get our attention and to draw us closer to you in the process.

GOD. *You are right, Kathy. I do allow things to come into your life for many different reasons. No matter what may come your way, always remember these words: Fear not, for I am with you; be not dismayed, for I am your God; I will strengthen you, I will help you, I will uphold you with my righteous right hand. Cast all your anxieties upon me because I care for you. Do not ever be afraid, and do not ever be discouraged. I knew that all of you involved would see me in this and that hearts would be forever changed.*

KATHY. I often use this event to gently help others understand that what they are complaining about carries little weight compared to what occurred on that day. The day-to-day things that cause us to complain must be put into perspective. Maybe that was your whole purpose for me. I will never know on this side of heaven, but I look forward to the day when you and I can have this conversation face to face.

GOD. *I look forward to that day as well, Kathy. Until then, keep encouraging those whom you come in contact with to seek me with the big and the small things. Those who wait for me shall renew their strength; they shall mount up like wings on eagles; they shall run and not grow weary; they shall walk and not faint.*

KATHY. That is one of my favorite verses, God. Thank you for that, and thank you for your endless mercies and blessings. Most of all, thank you for watching over Russell and for leaving him here with us a little longer. Love, Kathy.

Reflection of Today's Conversation

_____

_____

_____

_____

_____

Scripture Application

- God goes before us in every situation. He went before Russell on that tragic day and provided every single thing that would be needed to accomplish his perfect will in Russell's life. We can read in the scriptures where he went before the people who needed that extra ounce of protection.

- Trials were often experienced by God's people, but they all had a purpose. What we learn from the scriptures is that God is always in front of or behind, providing protection along the way. When the children of Israel were traveling out of the land of Egypt, God led them through the wilderness. Read *Exodus 13:21, 22.*

- Read *Exodus 14:13–31* to find out how the Lord went before the children of Israel and saved them. How did the people respond?
- Moses told Joshua he was to go with the people into the land God had promised them. Read *Deuteronomy 31:23* to find out how the Lord would go before them.
- Read *Matthew 28:16–20*. As Christ commissioned the disciples to go and make disciples of all nations, he reminded them that he would go before them and be with them to the end of the age. The Lord goes before us even today just as he went before Russell so many years ago. Let that thought resonate deep down in your heart, and as it does, it will be easier to *not* sweat the big or small stuff. God will take care of it all if only we will let him.

Wrap it Up

Kathy quoted the verses from James 1:2, 3 in this conversation, which clearly tells us to consider it all joy when we fall into various trials. It will never be easy for any of us to count it all joy when a trial comes our way, but God would not require anything of us that we could never achieve. Philippians 4:6,7 reminds us to

> Be anxious for nothing, but in everything
> by prayer and supplication with thanksgiving
> make our request known to God, and the peace
> of God, that passes all understanding will guard
> our minds and hearts through Christ Jesus.

That means in everything, leave it all at the feet of Jesus! I leave you with a quote from Oscar Wilde which so beautifully sums things up: "What seems to us as bitter trials are often blessings in disguise."

- Discussion
- Closing prayer

Father,

You remind us so often in your Word that you will never leave or forsake us. You are all-knowing and all-powerful, and you love us unconditionally. When trials come our way, keep us focused on you, and help us to understand that through it all, your perfect will is being accomplished in our lives. Because you are able to do exceedingly, abundantly above all that we could ever ask or think, we can rest in the fact that our lives are securely placed in your hands no matter what trial may come our way.

Amen

Consider it all joy when you fall into various trials, knowing that the testing of your faith produces patience.

—James 1:2, 3

Trials

A trial may come; a trial may go,
But this one thing,
God wants you to know.
He saw it first, he already knew,
The trail that was about
To happen to you.
He had a purpose, he had a plan,
To make and mold you
Into a better man.
If life were easy, around every turn,
There may be a lesson
You would never learn.
Lessons of discernment, in whatever you may face,

Lessons of dependence,
Upon God's sovereign grace.
God holds the future, your life is in his hands,
When you stumble or fall
He will gently help you stand.
A trial may come, yes, a trial may go,
But remember that is how
God will forever help you grow.

Kathy M. Crouch

CHAPTER 22

SIN

- Romans 3:23 ESV: *"All have sinned and fall short of the glory of God."*
- 1 John 1:9 ESV: *"If we confess our sins, he is faithful and just to forgive us our sins and cleanse us from all unrighteousness."*
- Romans 6:23 ESV: *"For the wages of sin is death, but the free gift of God is eternal life in Christ Jesus our Lord."*
- Psalm 103:12 ESV: *"As far as the east is from the west, so far does he remove our transgressions from us."*
- Isaiah 43:25 ESV: *"I am he who blots out your transgressions for my own sake, and I will not remember your sins."*

Let's Get Started

1. Webster defines *sin* as "an offence against religious or moral law; an action that is or is felt to be highly reprehensible." Billy Graham said, "A sin is any thought or action that falls short of God's will. God is perfect, and anything we do that falls short of his perfection is sin." What are your thoughts when it comes to sin?

2. As we know, Kathy loves to work in the yard and seems to hear God's voice there. Today she has a very unique way of comparing sin to yard work. Read *Romans 3:23*. Who

is exempt from sin? How do we receive God's glory if we fall short?

3.   Read *Romans 6:23*. What are the two realities in this verse? What do we learn about God's glory in these two verses?

4.   Read *1 John 1:9*. What miraculously happens when we realize we have sinned and confess it to God?

5.   Read *Psalm 103:12*. When we confess our sin to a holy God, what does he promise us he will do? Why should that bring us so much comfort?

6.   Read *Isaiah 43:25*. What is the power in this verse? Why, as humans, do we struggle with this truth? Do you think a person ever falls too far for God to forgive him/her? Why or why not?

A Conversation with God

KATHY. Dear God, whenever I tell my Sunday school students that I had another conversation with you, they immediately ask me whose yard I was working in. They have come to realize that I clearly hear your voice while I'm doing yard work. For reasons I can't explain, it's true, like today for instance. I heard you loud and clear through the leaves, sticks, pinecones, and weeds. I must say I am exhausted, but it was worth it.

GOD. *Yes, Kathy, I wasn't sure how you were going to connect those things to sin, but you managed to do it—quite effectively, if I must say so.*

KATHY. God, our sin is what led your precious son to Calvary. It is something that we can never take lightly. You tell us that we have all sinned and fallen short of your glory. No one is exempt. For some reason today, the leaves, pinecones, sticks, and weeds made me think about our sins.

GOD. *The wages of sin is death but the gift that I give is eternal life through my Son, Jesus. I have always known about sin and the effects of it. It began in the garden, and the only way to clean it up, which is where I think you are going next, was to offer up my son as a sacrifice for the sins of mankind.*

KATHY. So I was thinking about how once I became your child by receiving your free gift of salvation, the leaves, pinecones, and sticks remind me of the many yucky sins that have accumulated in my lifetime. Then under all of the leaves, pinecones, and sticks are the weeds. They just pop up everywhere. That's like after I confess all that I can remember, another one is there under the debris, and if I keep raking, confessing, more pop up.

GOD. *Do you know what I do once you confess a sin?*

KATHY. Yes, you forgive me of my sin and cleanse me of all unrighteousness.

GOD. *That's right, and I remember them no more. As far as the east is from the west, so far do I remove your transgressions from you. That is what happens after you dump all of the debris you have raked up in your yard. You don't have to go back to that pile year after year and rake up the same stuff. It is gone forever.*

KATHY. Yes, and that's what made me think of how new things fall from the trees each year and we are constantly raking. It's a never-ending cycle as long as we have trees and a yard. Sin will always be something I have to clean up because I am human and imperfect. Other sins will creep in, and I will need to confess them as well. It's a lot like yard work!

GOD. *If you don't wait until every leaf, pinecone, stick, or weed takes over your yard, it will be much more manageable. The same thing goes for sin.*

KATHY. I know what you mean. There is a section in my yard that I only clean up once a year. It is hidden behind a building so because I don't see it, I don't clean it until early spring. It is extremely hard to rake, and it's like everything has settled into the ground, making it difficult to remove. I guess that is like a sin in my life. The longer I let it stay, the harder it is to remember it and then confess it.

GOD. *That is a great analogy. When you do something that goes against my commandments, I will gently whisper in your ear and let you know. When you hear my voice, that will be the time to confess, repent, and turn. How do you feel after a hard day's work in that very large yard of yours?*

KATHY. I am so tired but happy at the same time. Everything is clean, the grass can be seen, and it gives me a great sense of accomplishment.

GOD. *That's how you should feel after you confess a sin to me. You should feel clean on the inside as if you had never sinned. As with yard work, don't wait to confess sins after they accumulate, but do it one sin at a time. I am holy. I cannot tolerate sin, and it will affect our relationship if it is not cleaned up. You can still enjoy your yard even if it hasn't been raked, but putting in the extra effort to clean it up will make spending time there even more enjoyable.*

KATHY. Lord, I am very thankful for this really big yard you have provided me with. I have always complained about the magnitude of just what falls from those trees. I have dreaded the task of the never-ending effort it takes to keep it tidy. Only you could have used this to teach me a lesson. I am so very thankful that you helped me see how sin can take over if it's not confessed on a regular basis; just like leaves, pinecones, sticks, and weeds, if not tended to, they can take over my yard. I will never again look at yard work the same.

GOD. *Kathy, I will always hear you when you come to me, whether it's in the yard or wherever you may be. Once you confess a sin, remember this. I am he who blots out your transgressions for my own sake, and I will not remember your sins. That should give you a reason to keep on raking.*

KATHY. Now *that* is a great analogy! You are an amazing God. I thank you and praise you for meeting me in the yard today to speak words of life and wisdom unto me once again. Love, Kathy.

Reflection of Today's Conversation

_____

_____

_____

_____

_____

_____

Scripture Application

- The *Webster Dictionary* defines a *parable* as "a usually short fictitious story that illustrates a moral attitude or a religious principle." Kathy's conversation concerning sin read much like one of the parables Jesus may have told. A parable uses everyday events and people to teach important lessons. Today we will take a look at two parables to dig a little deeper into the Scriptures and see how Jesus used stories to illustrate how delighted he is when just one sinner comes into his kingdom.
- In the first three verses of Luke 15, Jesus was talking to the tax collectors and sinners. The Pharisees and scribes grumble, saying, "This man receives sinners and eats with them." What are your thoughts?
- Jesus is eating with the very people who are lost and in need of a heart change. He begins to tell them just how lost they are in a very clever way. It's story time!
- Read *Luke 15:4–10*. These parables give us a clear vision of how much God loves us and how elated he is when just one sinner finds his way to him. Just as the Shepherd searches diligently for one lost sheep and the woman searches frantically for her lost coin, they both then celebrate it by sharing the good news with the people around them. God also celebrates when a lost soul is found.
- 2 Peter 3:9 says, "The Lord is not slow to fulfill his promise, as some count slowness; but is patient toward you, not wishing that any should perish, but that all should reach repentance." While we are waiting on his glorious return, what should we be searching for as Christians?
- Read *Romans 5:8*. One day I heard a lady say, "If you were the only person on this earth, Jesus would have died for you!" That comment spoke volumes to me. What are your thoughts?
- Read the very familiar passage once again, *John 3:16*. These verses carry so much weight! God sent his precious son to

die for our sins, and all we need to do to secure a place in heaven is to believe.

Wrap It Up

Sin entered the world in the garden, and it is still here with us today. First John 1:8 puts things into perspective as well as humbles us when it says, "If we claim to be without sin, we deceive ourselves and the truth is not in us." James 4:17 reminds us, "If anyone then knows the good they ought to do and doesn't do it, it is sin for them." I love the verse from the old hymn that says, "What can wash away our sins, nothing but the blood of Jesus." Jesus loves even the worst of sinners, but his desire is for us to confess our sins and repent so that he can do what he does best—forgive us our sins and cleanse us of all unrighteousness. Once we have done this, we should be seeking those who may have wandered from the faith, are lost, and are in need of the wonder-working power of our Lord and Savior, Jesus Christ.

- Discussion
- Closing prayer

Father,

We are all sinners saved by grace through grace plus nothing. Thank you for sending your son to take our sins upon himself on that cross at Calvary. Thank you that he rose on that third day and he lives so that we may live also. Bring every sin to our remembrance in the days ahead so that we may confess them and seek your forgiveness. May we be that light and salt you have called us to be in this dark world, and may we seek those who may be lost and lead them back to you.

Amen

And these will go away into eternal punishment,
but the righteous into eternal life.

—Matthew 25:46

Choice

Choice began in the garden
History was changed forever
Sinner, Listen
Satan
The ruler of darkness
Creator of lies
Destroyer
Sinner, Listen
God
Our Father in Heaven
Maker of all things
Savior
Sinner, Listen
Two choices
That's all we have
It began in the garden
It will end where we choose
Heaven or Hell
Choose wisely
It began in the garden
We will be there forever

Kathy M. Crouch

ABOUT THE AUTHOR

Kathy M. Crouch is a member of Crestview Baptist Church in Rockingham, North Carolina, where she has been a teacher of high school students for forty years. She retired from teaching first grade in 2009 after thirty years in the classroom. In 2012, she headed back to the classroom to help remediate struggling readers, and her first attempt at writing came in the form of a phonics initiative entitled *The Missing Link*. She was afforded the opportunity to implement this material throughout her county in grades K-5.

"God was indeed using this time to prepare me for this next journey," says Kathy. "I learned how to speak in front of people over the age of six, and believe me when I say I was terrified! He taught me how to write a curriculum and how to implement something of such magnitude. The knowledge and wisdom I gained from that experience helped me understand that it takes great humility to accomplish such a task. I had to learn to trust God and know that he often uses the least of these to accomplish his purposes. I consider myself just that—the least of these. As long as I knew that it was he who was doing all the work and I was just the vessel, everything ran smoothly. He was indeed preparing me for my next adventure, which would be *From the Master's Hand to Mine*."

Kathy has been happily married to her high school sweetheart for forty-three years. They have three children and seven precious grandchildren. You will meet many of them in the pages of her book. Kathy's hobbies include reading devotionals that inspire her, gardening, bringing old furniture back to life using chalk paint, and working in the yard. Kathy often says, "I tend to hear God's voice the loudest when I'm in the yard."